R.J. Haiman

I HATE TO SEE A MANAGER CRY

Or, How to Prevent the Litany of Management from Fouling up Your Career

BY MARTIN R. SMITH

Addison-Wesley Publishing Company
Reading, Massachusetts · Menlo Park, California · London · Don Mills, Ontario

Title page cartoon "All in line," from *Cartoons by Steinberg*, © Saul Steinberg. New York: Penguin Books, 1945.

Except for those who are obviously public personalities of the past or present, the characters mentioned in this book are composites, and have been given fictitious names, positions, and locations.

Copyright © 1973 by Addison-Wesley Publishing Company, Inc. Philippines copyright 1973 by Addison-Wesley Publishing Company, Inc.
All rights reserved. No part of this publication may be reproduced, stored in a retrieval system, or transmitted, in any form or by any means, electronic, mechanical, photocopying, recording, or otherwise, without the prior written permission of the publisher. Printed in the United States of America. Published simultaneously in Canada. Library of Congress Catalog Card No. 72-11258.

"Superstition, idolatry, and hypocrisy have ample wages; but truth goes a begging."
                    Martin Luther, "Table Talk," 1569

The Litany Of Management

This book is designed for managers and supervisors who are seeking the prizes of corporate success but who have come to recognize that the path to the executive suite is littered with the prostrate bodies of a multitude of unsuccessful contenders. Recognition of a treacherous path, however, is one thing; successful navigation of that same path is something else entirely.

These aspiring businessmen have searched assiduously for the right answers. They have read voluminously from the available legion of management improvement manuals; they have attended eagerly the countless seminars on management development.

Still, the prize is elusive. Something, these men feel, is missing. Something important. They are genuinely puzzled, for the endless chain of texts and lectures on achieving corporate success has not proved beneficial to their careers. These men are at a loss. They have sincerely attempted to apply the golden rules to their jobs, but they have failed.

If you are one of these persons, stop right now and wipe away that self-defeating attitude! The failure is not yours. It is instead the misleading, deceptive, and hypocritical litany of the management theorists that is damaging your career. *The worst possible error made by men who seek to improve their business performance through study is to believe all the junk prescribed by lecturers and texts on achieving management success.* Inevitably, writers and lecturers mouth the same trite formulas based on the existing value system. In one form or another they advise you to be:

Poised	Patient
Confident	Assured
Persuasive	Energetic
Dynamic	Sociable
Thoughtful	Accurate

Enthusiastic	Sympathetic
Aggressive	Precise
Discreet	Enterprising
Practical	Polished
Courageous	Cautious
Deliberate	Dignified
Modest	Systematic
Steady	And so on———

If that isn't enough to confuse already befuddled persons, they offer the following golden rules (or variants of them) for achievement of executive success:

1. Be nice to people
2. Learn technical competence
3. Don't pass the buck
4. Admit your mistakes
5. Give credit where due
6. Act inspired
7. Communicate well
8. Plan ahead
9. Be loyal
10. Think

Unsuspecting managers who allow themselves to be influenced by all of this are not only headed for ignominy but they are liable to become raving idiots to boot. Even if it were possible to assimilate and practice all of these rules, they are no guarantee of success. In fact, they are misleading if only because they neglect to establish the hard core business realities—the way things really are.

Please don't feel insulted or ashamed for having tried your lot with the prevailing conventional wisdom. Most people suffer through it. I did myself. Now, several years later, after learning to recognize many of the common fallacies, I feel it is time to debunk the management theories.

There are several names used to describe the management success phenonemon: "The conventional wisdom," "The folklore of management," "The theories of good management," etc. My own name for it is: *"The Litany of Management."* By definition, "litany" means a repetitive recitation. When applying it to the word "management," it describes the ineffectual responses of businessmen to the repetitive, omnipresent rules of management success as prescribed by the so-called seers of the business community. The men who spread this gospel arise from business, government, and the academic world. Perpetuators of the litany of management, it seems, are everywhere. From their prolific pens flow books and courses of study designed to "help" businessmen correct weaknesses or develop strengths—and the flood grows year after year. And yet they all ignore the real truths. Damned few of them, for example, tell you how to counteract the thrusts of a clever infighter, *the guy who is after your job any way he can get it.* These same theorists invariably claim that a good administrator can move from industry to industry, the power of his organizational thrust outweighing his product knowledge or technical competence. Yet, a rigid, unthinking belief in this rule has been the downfall of many good men. In another instance, adherence to that litany which claims that a pat on the back carries more weight than a pat on the paycheck has shattered the beliefs of many managers and irreversibly damaged their careers.

I could go on and on. But after all, that's the purpose of this book. For fifteen years I've observed and participated in corporate life at succeeding levels of management. My experience has been that of an insider. I haven't been required to imagine what went on behind those closed doors because I was there myself, participating actively. I've managed functions in production, quality control, industrial engineering, and production control, besides completing work assignments in many other areas of business. I was associated for a period of time with a national management consulting firm which gave me access to many other corporations along with the opportunity to watch and analyze corporate businessmen in action. I am still very active in consulting work, this time on my own, besides conducting full-day seminars around the country in effective management techniques. All of this has given me the rare opportunity of working closely with senior- and middle-level management people on a wide variety of business problems.

Shortly after embarking on my business career I began to discover the sham and hypocrisy of the litany of management. The lessons were painful at first, but quickly I learned what the business code was really all about. Then last year I read Robert Townsend's "Up the Organization," and I was overjoyed to realize that, finally, a fresh and honest wind had blown across the stale wastelands of the Litany of Management. While I was particularly gratified to see his book in print, I realized that little had been written for the student, trainee, supervisor, and middle-level manager using the Townsend approach. So here we are.

Some of the experiences related in this book I have observed firsthand; the rest are all my own. Hard-earned experiences, in some cases, but I'm grateful to the many superiors and associates who over the years have given me the opportunity to acquire them—men who not only have mastered the real arts of management but who also have had the ability to stand back and laugh at the business game as they played it. I believe that many of these men have discovered the secret.

M.R.S.

Somerville, N.J.
October 1972

Acknowledgments

Unlike Robert Townsend, I do have a secretary and I would like to thank her—Mrs. Joanne Del Rocco—for typing the manuscript of this book. Above all I acknowledge the help and friendship I received from many associates over the years, most particularly: Mike, Howard, Chuck, Jack, and Jim. I would like also to mention that the views expressed in this book are not necessarily shared by these men.

Martin R. Smith

Test Your Management Skills

Before you read this book, before you even glance through the contents, take the following three-minute test. There are no tricks involved. The test is designed simply to give you a brief indication of your knowledge of management functions.

Answer each question True or False

1. My career potential is limited mostly by the amount of work I am willing to do. The manager who works hard has a better chance for success than the manager who doesn't.

2. Management objectives are best handled by assigning specific goals to a team. The team itself is composed of people with specific skills needed to tackle the goals.

3. A manager with administrative skills can handle most managerial jobs provided that his staff possesses the needed technical knowledge.

4. Image (size, weight, manner of dress, bearing) are not related to success on the job.

5. Performance evaluations should concentrate on indicating and overcoming weaknesses that hinder performance.

6. A good manager should make himself available to his staff both nights and weekends to help them reach important decisions.

7. Money is important to people, but there are other considerations that are more important.

8. The boss should almost always display a no-nonsense, all business demeanor.

9. If a manager is careful about interviewing applicants for a job, he can be sure he is gaining a good employee almost every time.

10. Effectiveness is the ability to do a job right.

11. Establishing a program to combat a specific ailment of the organization is a logical, orderly way of attacking problems.

12. Psychological testing is a generally effective way to screen job applicants.

13. Bureaucracy is a problem normally associated with government functions.

14. Office politics can be virtually eradicated if the proper approach is taken by top management.

15. Experience in production may not be particularly useful for the staff-oriented individual. Production functions are too divorced from staff work to be of any significant utility.

16. Decisions on how to handle details are best left to the manager's staff.

17. Management jargon serves a particularly useful purpose. It allows members of a specialty group to communicate effectively with other members of the organization.

18. Titles are not important. It's the money that counts.

19. In our democratic society, fringes such as reserved parking spaces and dining room privileges are more a social detriment than an economic privilege, and should be discontinued.

20. Written memoranda should replace face-to-face conversation whenever possible. The written word is not as subject to misinterpretation.

Now that you have completed this test, please turn to the next page to see how you scored.

Test answers

The answer to every question on the test you have just taken is "false." If you answered one, several, or all of them "true," don't become dismayed or alarmed. You're probably a supervisor or manager who has concentrated his efforts on mastering his job and you have sincerely applied your knowledge for the joint benefit of your career objectives and company goals. That is highly commendable.

But don't let it throw you off the track.

The well-meaning person who, having played poker a few times, allows himself to be conned into sitting down with hard-eyed strangers for a friendly game, is headed for disaster. The businessman who has worked in organizations for a few years is in a somewhat parallel situation. He has had enough experience to consider himself competent to play the management game, but not as much as he may think. Whether he knows it or not, he has drawn cards at a table where the hardest, most complicated, and perhaps the most demanding game is being played for high stakes—those stakes being the businessman's job and future. It is a certainty that any businessman who lacks intimate understanding of the way the game is played will be a loser.

This implies that "working smart" is more critical to your chances of success than "working hard." It is also, indirectly, the answer to the first question of the test: "My career potential is limited mostly by the amount of work I am willing to do. The manager who works hard has a better chance for success than the manager who doesn't."

The other questions are answered in sections listed on the following page.

Question	Section	Page
2	Management by objectives	181
3	Job knowledge vs. administrative skills	153
4	Do you look like an executive?	139
5	Appraisal techniques that build managers	178
6	Decision-making at home	155
7	Paychecks come first	120
8	Keep your sense of humor	164
9	Hiring people	173
10	Effectiveness vs. efficiency	183
11	Programitis	4
12	Beating the God-players	59
13	Weeding out bureaucracy and deadwood	6
14	Sizing up the cutthroat	45
15	Put them all in production	147
16	Details are important	152
17	Address yourself to plumbers	159
18	Titles are important	134
19	Fringes for the foreman too	121
20	How *not* to write memos	67

Now read on to see how this book can help you evaluate business situations realistically and avoid the common pitfalls.

Contents

PART ONE: RECOGNIZING MANAGEMENT DISEASES   2

Programitis: a management disease   4

Weeding out bureaucracy and deadwood   6

Seconds-in-command: a no-no   10

Professional societies have an obligation   12

Safety can't wait   14

Traveling for the company, or, booze and broads vs. business   17

Monthly reports   20

Overconfidence   21

The detective instinct at work   23

Credulousness   27

Obtainable goals   29

Promises, promises   31

Managers and mistresses   33

Socializing with your people   35

Zero defects and other slices of baloney, or, achieving product quality   36

PART TWO: CIRCUMVENTING CORPORATE POLITICS   40

Ethics in business?   42

Sizing-up the cutthroat: guerilla warfare   45

Infighting   49

Compatibility with the boss   54

Angels   57

Beating the God-players, or, dehumanizing management through personality tests   59

Meeting style for the careful manager (POOP)   63

Conference style   65

How not to write memos   67

Skirmishing tactics   69

Swatting flies   73

PART THREE: HANDLING CORPORATE PERSONALITIES   76

Corporate do-gooders   77

Purists at work   81

Numbers men, or, don't fall prey to the statisticians   83

High priests of the computer room   87

Craftsmen can be costly   90

The cluttered desk phony   93

The research man syndrome   95

Secretaries   98

PART FOUR: DEBUNKING ACCEPTED PERSONNEL THEORIES   102

People and personnel   103

Management training   110

Democratic management?   112

The fallacies in theory Y   114

Scrooge and the pay raise   118

Paychecks come first   120
Fringes for the foremen, too   121
It's a man's world   122
Blacks in business   126

PART FIVE: GETTING THERE: SELECTING THE RIGHT JOB   130

Mating of man and company   131
Titles are important   134
Do you like your company's products?   136
Do you look like an executive? or, the importance of image   139
Transfer happy   142

PART SIX: STAYING THERE: TECHNIQUES FOR SUCCESS   146

Put them all in production   147
Dealing with unions: the only way   149
Details are important   152
Job knowledge vs. administrative skills   153
Some thoughts on mistakes   154
Decision-making at home, or, Ma Bell and me   155
Every manager a salesman   156
Address yourself to plumbers, or, words and phrases that hamper communication   159
Treat them equally   162
Keep your sense of humor   164
Hero yesterday, bum tomorrow   166
Avoid emotional reactions   167
Books on management development   169

PART SEVEN: MOVING AHEAD: DOING THE RIGHT THINGS 172

Hiring people 173

Selecting the best people for promotion 175

Firing people 176

Appraisal techniques that build managers 178

The final step in behavioral correction 180

Management by objectives 181

Effectiveness vs. efficiency: a world of difference 183

Leave a path open 185

Demand excellence 187

Send out a scout 188

Tight budgets are best 189

Time 190

Short-interval scheduling: a tool for all managers 191

Now that you're on your way 193

PART EIGHT: NOW TEST YOURSELF AGAIN— 196

EPILOGUE: I HATE TO SEE A MANAGER CRY 208

Part One
RECOGNIZING MANAGEMENT DISEASES

It is a fact that more businessmen lose their jobs, not because they lack technical expertise, but for their failure to recognize the pitfalls inherent in organizations.

A well-known management consultant

To understand how to cope with the dangers inherent in the litany of management, you must first learn how to recognize them. Some are as obvious as the dry and stale movements of an ossified management; others are quite subtle and difficult to perceive. To begin with, recognize the fact that corporate halls are inundated with unrewarding and utterly fruitless concepts, policies, ideas, practices, and goals. To the untrained and unsuspecting eye, nothing could be further from the truth; the initial exposure to the corporate world normally gives the opposite impression entirely. Serious looking men hurriedly stride from office to office, their expressions intent, papers jammed in hand. Offices overflow with people rushing in many different directions, doing many important-looking things. Telephones ring insistently and small groups of hard-eyed men converge in meeting rooms to thrash out seemingly momentous problems. Everywhere there is action. A sense of purpose permeates the atmosphere. To the new man, this entire panorama is exciting, fascinating. It evokes visions of accomplishment and satisfaction.

But the glance from a trained eye thrusts deeper. It moves below the surface phenomena to observe the real workings. It takes nothing for granted. All of the movement, all of the talk, all of the actions are stripped bare. Real motivation is contrasted to surface motivation. Penetrating questions are asked.

And the answers are sometimes painful.

The intent man hurrying down the corridor is on his way to a coffee break. The intelligent-looking woman is struggling to compose a report that nobody will ever read. The supervisors who are wrestling with issues in the conference room will decide nothing concrete. The entire movement that we see is mostly facade—those people are either concentrating on fulfillment of their own personal desires or, more than likely, doing their jobs improperly.

Newcomers to corporate halls must learn that many corporate actions perpetuated by most corporate beings are futile and unproductive. They must recognize the management diseases described on the following pages. Businessmen who are genuinely interested in advancing their careers will find identification of these diseases to be of particular benefit.

Programitis: A Management Disease

There is an enervating disease spreading through corporate corridors today which strikes predominantly among middle managers. This infectious disease is called "Programitis."

Whenever problems face management, someone somewhere along the line suggests "a program." It doesn't make any difference whether the problem is faltering sales, soaring production costs, clerical bottlenecks, or malfunctioning equipment. The solution to many managers appears deceptively simple: Start a program.

The very core and essence of "Programitis" is the sometimes conscious, sometimes unconscious fear of any single manager to tackle the problem at hand and lick it. It represents corporate maneuvering at its peak; the shirking of responsibility and the diffusion of time, attention, thought, and skills. For example: A plant is experiencing a major quality problem with one of its product lines. Does the Quality Control Manager marshal the needed talent and dig into the tooling, material specifications, operator training, and work methods? Many times, unfortunately not. Why should the Quality Control Manager put himself on the spot and assume responsibility for results? Instead, he forms a committee and initiates a Zero Defects or Quality Certification program. That way *everyone* involved can share in the blame if the program falls apart at the seams. There is a great deal of comfort and safety under the protective blanket of group decisions. Nobody exposes himself unduly. Of course, the problem may not get solved, or the solution may be slow in coming, or it may turn out to be the wrong solution altogether.

Programitis is sometimes an unintentional by-product of today's burgeoning systems technology. The idea of attacking problems through well-formulated mathematical programs such as Operations Research and Linear Programming has its values, and many of these mathematical tools are marvelously attuned to solving unique problems. But it's ridiculous to use the program approach to tackle all or most of management's problems. Nothing gets done.

There is one very dependable way of choking off and defeating Programitis. Set an objective to achieve a specific goal and make one individual responsible for the attainment of that objective. Establish a mutually agreeable time limit for its completion, allowing just enough time to do a good job but not enough time to establish standing committees, programs, and other methods of avoiding responsibility. You can rest assured that any ambitious and intelligent manager will knock down doors to get the job done. Particularly when he is aware that meeting the goal is *his* baby.

Now stand back and watch him burn up the trails. With your help and guidance, the goal will be made and the objective achieved. Even better, your manager will have grown in stature, both in your eyes and his. The greatest motivation tool available for a manager is success. Knowing that he is capable of solid performance, he will move on to the next opportunity with acres of self-confidence.

Weeding Out Bureaucracy and Deadwood

What happens when a new job is created? Well, at the outset, it's budgeted at salary plus a few incidental expenses. A man is placed in the job. Before long he has to have a secretary, furniture, equipment, supplies, etc. These accessories soon create so much work for him that he has to have an assistant. Then, in due time, the assistant has to have a secretary, furniture, equipment—and so it goes. Before we know it, some clerks have been added and the "job" has been transformed into a department.

As improbable as this may sound, it is seen everywhere: business, industry, government, academe.

A company I know of, a small division of a major consumer products company, packaged its own products. A few highly specialized packaging machines were used for this purpose. The company depended on the maker of the packaging machinery to supply it with the engineering skills needed to keep the machinery operating. This arrangement proved cumbersome and eventually the company made a decision to hire its own mechanical engineer with experience in packaging machinery.

The budget addition was approved and the man was hired. It wasn't too long after he started that he decided it was necessary to purchase some highly automated electro-mechanical testing equipment to analyze machine problems. This too was approved, and the equipment was purchased.

After the new equipment was put in use, the engineer found he was spending so much time analyzing machine deficiencies that he was not paying attention to other important parts of his job. Consequently, he sold his boss on the idea of hiring a technician to operate the testing equipment.

Not long after that a machinist was hired to implement the machine design changes recommended by the engineer. Soon

the engineer found himself so busy with paperwork that a secretary-clerk had to be added to the payroll to relieve him of that task.

Within two years after the company had hired an engineer to perform a very specific task, it had established an Engineering Machinery Department with a budget of six people and an expensive testing laboratory to maintain. This, mind you, supplanted the free services provided by the packaging machinery manufacturer!

Now a strange thing happened in the meantime. When the function was initially established and when additional people and equipment were added, there was a lot of grumbling about cost justification by the financial men and one or two of the vice-presidents. But after another year or so this grumbling actually ceased. What happened was that people became so accustomed to having the Engineering Machinery Department as part of the organization that they stopped questioning its existence. It was now a fully accepted member of the organization, and neither the old-timers nor the new people joining the company thought twice about its reason for being.

That's bureaucracy, and while it is less controllable and less impeded in government, its elements are inherent in every type of organization.

It is the responsibility of every manager to ruthlessly eliminate functions that do not contribute to profits. He does this by asking himself: "What does the department contribute to the company?" And if the answer does not meet expectations, then the function must be removed. And quickly, before it attains acceptability in the organization.

The manager cannot question only the new function. He must look around him and question severely the legitimacy of *all* existing functions. Many organizations today have "Engineering Machinery Departments"; most of these functions have been around for so long that people automatically accept them as necessary, when in fact they are not.

The manager's task is not an easy one. It takes some very hard thinking coupled with the ability to make hard-nosed decisions to cut off a job, or even an entire department. Needless to say, the justification for doing that must be sold to top management. This stage separates the men from the boys. Remember, somebody upstairs has a vested interest in the jobs under question. Either some vice-president created the function being questioned, or he approved of its inception. In any case, he is not likely to admit readily that he made a stupid mistake. The manager who bucks him could easily incur the wrath of a potentially dangerous enemy. So his job is a tough one, indeed. It takes diplomacy, thought, and just plain guts. But *somebody* must do it. Otherwise the organization will strangle itself on its own excessive, noncompetitive costs.

How can the manager spot organizational fat in his own department? If the jobs in his area have been time-studied, the task is easy. Using the standard rates and allowances he can build up a workload on the basis of actual work accomplished, and see for himself how much time is being devoted to departmental goals.

If the jobs haven't been subjected to time study, the task is immeasurably more difficult. The manager may at first want time studies made of the work, but this may not be practical for many reasons. The manager may be working with a salaried group, for example, and any attempt to develop workloads may lead to unionization. His only recourse is to study the signs of deadwood, and later make a decision concerning individual jobs.

How is that done?

There are certain signs to observe. A careful examination of the jobs may reveal the following indications of growing organizational fat:

a) Many of the individual tasks being performed can be totally eliminated.

b) Many of the individual tasks being performed can be combined with other tasks or can be absorbed by another person.

c) Records indicate a heavy and continuous overtime schedule on non-time-studied jobs.

d) An inordinate amount of time is spent on any one step (or series of steps) in the work flow. This is an indication that there are too many steps in the work flow.

e) Too many people are devoting a large proportion of their time to putting out fires. A lean, well-run organization is comparatively dull, because work has been adequately organized and there are only a few fires to be put out.

f) Frequently missed schedules are commonplace.

Contrary to popular belief, the over-staffed organization does not get out more work than the leaner organization. People devote their time to the wrong tasks in the fat department, and they are constantly tripping over each other. There are just too damn many of them. If you recognize any of these symptoms in your organization, you have your work cut out for you. Chances are you can tighten your belt a hefty notch or two.

Seconds-In-Command: A No-No!

The use of line assistants must be evaluated carefully before allowing them a place in the organization. Look at it this way: If the manager leaves the department, the assistant manager will expect to take over. That's fine provided the assistant is capable. If he's not, you've got a real headache. Promoting someone else over his head will probably force the assistant to quit. Maybe that's what is best under the circumstances, but why put him in that position to begin with? If he is a capable man as a supervisor, why not keep him working at that job? As long as he is an able contributor, he is fulfilling his purpose. Surely, when the time comes, a manager can select the best of his supervisors to be promoted without first creating an assistant manager's job to test a man.

One of the real dangers of creating an assistant's spot is that an individual looks and acts in a very different way when he is on his own than he does when he is assisting someone else. For example, you may decide that Joe is the man to replace Gary as the department head when Gary retires next year. Therefore you make Joe Gary's assistant. During the year you observe Joe closely. From time-to-time you are inclined to doubt your original judgment because he looks weak, he does not seem to be in command of himself or the organization. You begin to have serious doubts. Joe does not appear to have the strength you thought he had.

You make hasty arrangements and transfer Joe to another part of the organization. He is still working as an assistant department head, but in a different department. Now and then you hear reports about Joe. His performance is still decidedly lackluster.

Without advance warning Joe's boss quits. The department is without a leader. Higher management is in a spot and decides to take a chance on Joe. He becomes manager of the department.

After a few weeks everyone is astounded. You wonder just what the hell happened to Joe. He is another person entirely; he seems to know exactly what to do and he's doing it well—far better, in fact, than you originally expected he could.

The answer is simple, even obvious. An individual cannot show to his best advantage unless he has full responsibility. Something happens to him when he takes over. He is no longer carrying out responsibilities under detailed instructions from another. Now he is exercising his own judgment and his own capabilities; he knows that he must measure up because only he is accountable. He has become a dynamic and effective leader.

It is extremely difficult to rate the performance of a second-in-command. But there is one time when his existence is justified. That occurs when the manager is a short time from retirement or transfer and his replacement has already been selected from the supervisors' ranks. The job that the new man can do is well known, and placing him as assistant manager for a few years will do no harm—provided that at the end of that time the new man becomes the manager.

As a rule, seconds-in-command should not be used as a standing part of the organization. Until a man becomes number one you can never be 100 percent positive about him. Most certainly, you'll never find out by making him the number two man.

Professional Societies Have an Obligation

Professional societies were established by members of unique specialty groups, primarily to advance the state of the art of the specialty and upgrade the professional status of its members. For the most part these efforts have been successful, and the societies have contributed greatly to the business community-at-large.

There has been an unhealthy by-product, however. In recent years particularly, professional societies have displayed tendencies to foster many inbred specialists. Some members of the specialty groups have come to feel that mastery of their art or science is an end in itself. They appear to enclose themselves in a protective cocoon of technical sophistication and communicate with each other through a babble of technical jargon that is unintelligible to the outsider. Words and phrases such as "regression equations," "third-generation feasibility studies" and the like waft through the air, generated by prideful pros.

If you have ever attended any of the regional meetings or national conventions of these groups, then you know what I mean. Often there is quite obviously a pervasive attitude of, let me say it, smugness. The basic impression received by detached visitors is: "My art or science is bigger and better than your art or science." Similarly, "Those crude people in production could never begin to understand my specialty."

By far the most onerous result of this attitude has been inbreeding—the population of business with narrow and rigid specialists. Inevitably these super-specialists are so wrapped up in their tightly circumscribed world that they are unable to contribute substantially to company efforts. The eternal business truths, sales and profits, mean nothing to these people; they would be hard put to relate their given activity to increases in either sales or profits.

They have lost sight of the goal. And because they have, businessmen are beginning to shun them. I personally believe that many of the scientists and engineers who were layed off during the recession of 1970 lost their jobs because company managements used the excuse of poor business to clear their houses of deadwood. I do not think all of the layoffs were caused by slower economic conditions.

It would be unfair to blame the professional societies entirely for the dismal perspective of many of their members. Undoubtedly, much of the fault can be traced to the poor attitudes of many engineers and scientists. But the professional societies do have an obligation to the business community because they command huge memberships. It is now up to them to redirect the thinking of their memberships into broader channels and provide business with specialists who are willing and able to contribute to management goals.

Safety Can't Wait

Several years ago I worked in production for the sheet metal division of a major automotive company. As general foreman in charge of production for the department, I managed a three-shift operation where hoods and fenders for all of the division's automobiles were fabricated. If you have ever worked in the automotive industry then you can readily visualize the atmosphere: tough, demanding, hard-nosed, and production-oriented. Primary emphasis was placed on getting the work out, and God help that hapless soul who fell behind the production schedule.

The jobs in my department were physically tough and demanding for the operators and helpers who manned the presses. For them the job consisted of positioning a preformed fender inside a press, cycling the press, then removing the fender and handing it on to the next operator at the adjacent work station. Each fender weighed about 30 pounds, and in the course of one shift each operator would normally handle about 2000 fenders.

It took younger men to handle the operators' jobs, and since they would always seek work of a less demanding nature, our turnover was high. This was a perpetual headache which resulted in lost production and high training costs. Since the job of safety training belonged to the foreman, it sometimes took a back seat to the recurring daily pressures of production.

One Tuesday evening at 11:55, Jimmy C., a press operator, reported for his stint on the midnight shift. Having celebrated his 19th birthday earlier that day, Jimmy was quite euphoric—in fact he was plain drunk. When he arrived at his press several of his co-workers laughed at Jimmy's bleary eyes and whiskey-laden breath. His foreman was too preoccupied with shift startup duties to notice anything unusual about him.

About one hour into the shift, after the rhythm of production had been established and the operators were settled down to the night's work, Jimmy had a great idea. Rather than wait another 10 minutes for a scheduled cigarette break, he would have one now. But in order to do this, he would need to free one of his hands both of which were occupied on the dual hand buttons needed to actuate the press. The purpose of dual buttons is obvious; if an operator must keep both hands on the buttons to cycle the press, there is no way he can inadvertently get a hand caught between its steel jaws. This is an old and reliable safety device, having been used in the press industry for many years. But it can be circumvented (just like any other safety device in existence) if someone wants to circumvent it. Jimmy wanted to—and did. Getting a key from the area electrician, he locked out one of the buttons and lit a cigarette. Now he could actuate the press with one hand and enjoy his smoke at the same time.

A drunk kid working a dangerous piece of equipment without adequate safety control is a potential time bomb. As you can sadly guess, the bomb went off. At exactly 1:25 a.m. Jimmy discarded the half-smoked cigarette, feeling momentarily dizzy. His left hand moved to the sole remaining button to cycle the press and at that very moment the operator adjacent to him called to Jimmy to get the next fender. As Jimmy later revealed, at the moment of the accident he had been "soaring," then suddenly he got dizzy, and when his name was called out he pivoted to the side, slipped, and his right hand shot out for support. It landed on the lower half of the press jaws a split second after his left hand actuated the press.

Jimmy's scream of agony echoed throughout the entire pressroom. When he instinctively jerked his right arm from the press there was no hand attached. Dazed and shocked, he looked at the press and saw the grisly remains of his right hand. The horrifying truth penetrated, and he fainted.

The following evening the foreman in charge of the shift submitted his resignation and I accepted it. It was one of the toughest decisions I've ever made. Harsh? Yes. You say possibly there were extenuating circumstances? Maybe. Weren't both Jimmy and the electrician responsible? After all, they broke safety regulations.

Well, that's entirely correct. But Jimmy was already punished more than enough and the electrician was later disciplined for giving him the lock-out key.

The foreman, however, had not provided adequate basic safety training for Jimmy—as well as other new operators. He also was responsible for detecting Jimmy's stuporous condition *before* Jimmy was assigned to his job that night. Granted, he was under the pressure of his job, but it's a matter of perspective. Human life and limb *must* be protected before other matters are considered; namely production, quality, and cost. Safety *must* come first. It can't wait, and unfortunately, until some tragic event occurs, people have a real hard time understanding that essential fact.

Because of Jimmy, it's stamped on my mind indelibly.

Traveling for the Company,
or
Booze and Broads vs. Business

Sooner or later most businessmen are exposed to some company-sponsored travel. For most people this represents a welcome break in the routine. Whatever the reason for the trip, sales convention or plant visitation, most people enjoy the change of pace.

Trouble starts when they enjoy it too much.

There are a multitude of "good time Charlies" on the road. My own experience—and I have traveled literally millions of miles on company business—has led me to this conclusion: It is virtually impossible to keep travelers, particularly travelers with generous expense accounts, out of the bars and in the public libraries. It is totally unrealistic to expect that a businessman will use his free time at night to probe the hidden meanings of Schopenhauer at the local philosophical society. Those are tales for the wives. After a full day of travel and work, the guy is exhausted and very ready for a soothing and relaxing dry martini—maybe two.

What happens then? He becomes so damned relaxed after those two drinks that he decides to have dinner and then spend just twenty minutes or so at the bar having one more. Well, three hours and twenty minutes later he is positively euphoric and ready for anything that might come his way. And what do you think he wants to come his way? A broad. And those found alone at cocktail lounges are usually in the same psychological circumstances as company travelers. Ready for anything.

It can only lead to trouble and it inevitably does.

The entire convoluted mess can best be summed up by Smith's formula: $Tr = AA + 1LT + 1LW + 5B$,
where
TR = trouble,
AA = alien atmosphere (nobody knows you),
1LT = one lonely traveler, hot for action,
1LW = one local woman, hot for action,
5 B = about five parts booze (catalyst).

This concoction can and does create trouble simply because: (1) the guy's wife is going to find lipstick on his clothes or long hair in his comb, (2) the company is going to discover that its fair-haired boy is more interested in broads and booze than business, (3) the gal's husband or boyfriend will come looking for her.

There are some time-tested ways to stay out of trouble on the road:
1. Travel with your boss or your peers.
2. Work late, eat dinner late and confine yourself to *one* drink.

3. Have dinner with some of the company's local men—preferably at their homes.
4. Plan something you enjoy at night like taking in a show.
5. Even better, send me your little black book. I'm going to Minneapolis next Thursday.

Monthly Reports

There are two types of monthly reports. First are those containing numerical data such as sales, costs, and quality defect levels, where monthly or even weekly and daily information is needed to control segments of the business. Their purpose is wholly legitimate and necessary.

Second are those which are essentially progress reports describing a certain department's activities for the month. Frankly, these are pure, unadulterated bullshit and should be ruthlessly eliminated. Reports of this kind are subject to the space-fill phenomenon described originally by C. N. Parkinson. This law states that periodic progress reports required by management will be written whether or not the authors have anything pertinent to say. The fertile imagination of authors, desperate to fill space, occasionally yields such ridiculous results as this excerpt from a purchasing agent's monthly report:

"Efforts were continued to obtain an alternate supplier for our paperboard covers. On April 17, Bob Jones and myself had dinner with Mr. Paul Fredricks, President and Owner of Federal Paper Products. I can personally state that inroads were made during the meal. Mr. Fredricks, in fact, told me afterwards that the lobster he had for dinner was the best he ever had. He left the meal quite contented and I think we can look forward to Mr. Fredrick's supplying us with the folders that we need."

Periodic progress reports inevitably waste time. Besides the author who sweats out filling empty space with empty words, there are the frustrated readers who are impatiently attempting to glean the information they need from ten pages of rubbish.

The best single way to handle project reports is to issue a one-page summary at the conclusion of the project. Do not permit a single written word to be distributed until then. Keep your people away from pencil-pushing and they won't have to fabricate written excuses every month. They'll spend that time doing their jobs instead.

Overconfidence

Managers sometimes get so full of themselves that they consider themselves to be omniscient. This happens particularly when they have scored three or four back-to-back successful deals on the job. They radiate the "I can't lose" feeling. When this occurs, these managers are headed for serious trouble. They are riding the crest but they are unaware of the wave gathering behind them, preparing to knock their wind out and send them tumbling.

Don't confuse overconfidence with confidence. The successful manager knows where he is going and can make others want to go with him. That's confidence. However, when he gets so cocky that he feels nothing can go wrong, that's overconfidence, and it's potentially just as dangerous to managers as booze is to drivers.

When I started as a consultant, my superior told me, "Your main stock in trade is confidence. Always give the impression of knowing exactly what you are doing, even when you are not sure at all. And always radiate confidence most when things are going badly."

He then went on to say, "That doesn't mean that you shouldn't be fully and objectively aware of what's really happening. On the contrary, the more success you have, the closer you want to examine what you are doing. That's the time to slow down deliberately and very carefully question yourself about every phase of the project. The cardinal sin of the consultant is to allow too much success to interfere with his normally good judgment."

I believe those words can be applied to any manager in any line of business. To disregard them is an invitation to disaster. One sales manager told of having negotiated two very large and very profitable contracts for his company. As he put it, "I was riding right on top. It seemed as if I had the golden touch. Then: Whammo! I got it, and got it good!" Careless from overconfidence, he entered into a third contract without carefully understanding the distribution costs, which in this case, were prohibitive. The result was a loss that wiped out almost all of the profits of the two preceding deals.

Whenever you feel that lady luck is on your side—that nothing can go wrong—that is the time to bang your ego-swelled head against the wall and start thinking realistically. It's the time to devote extra time and care to your decisions.

The Detective Instinct at Work

One of today's master writers of detective novels is Ross McDonald. In *The Underground Man*, *The Goodbye Look*, and several other novels, McDonald has displayed extraordinary perception of how people get into hopeless entanglements. He created the cool and pragmatic private investigator, Lew Archer. Archer's ability to dig and ferret out every involved detail until he has unravelled the motivation behind events is the great strength he uses to solve all of his cases.

Archer, in other words, never accepts things at face value. He investigates relentlessly until the combination of facts he has discovered satisfies and explains events on hand.

It strikes me that the detective instinct, so ably illustrated by McDonald via Archer, is one of the true needs of the corporate manager. Neglecting to understand figures, accepting motivation too casually, taking a laissez-faire attitude toward facts—all of these presage failure. They outline the modus operandi of the manager who will miss opportunities, or lose his job, because he didn't use his detective instinct.

Let's examine the detective instinct at work.

A Sales Manager for an electronics firm found that sales for the East Coast were $130,000 below the quota of $14,500,000 for the first six months of 1972. Actual sales were $14,370,000. The quota was based on forecasted sales of the various types of electronic components manufactured by the company, more specifically on forecasts by the product group in each factory for each salesman's territory.

The Sales Manager was not too concerned over the small drop in sales. It amounted to 1.5 percent, and he was inclined to forget the matter, particularly since sales forecasts err to some extent. He started to put the matter aside, and then, almost instinctively, he returned to the sales figures, scrutinizing them carefully. Table 1 shows what they looked like.

	Thousands of dollars		Performance
Area	Quota	Actual	Actual/Quota
New York	$ 4,675	$ 4,765	102%
Boston	3,625	3,675	101%
Washington	3,000	2,800	93%
Philadelphia	3,200	3,130	98%
Totals	$14,500	$14,370	99%

The Sales Manager hesitated. All areas looked fairly good, although Washington was down slightly. He decided to investigate further. The salesmen's figures for the Washington area broke down as shown in Table 2.

	Thousands of dollars		Performance
Salesman	Quota	Actual	Actual/Quota
Jones	$ 750	$ 780	104%
Ferguson	800	550	69%
Perkins	790	840	106%
Ambrose	660	630	95%
Totals	$3,000	$2,800	93%

The Sales Manager was amazed. Historically, Ferguson had been the top salesman in the Eastern area. Something very obviously was wrong. He was gratified that he had followed his intuition and investigated further.

Now he was confronted with a real problem. What should he do now? Why had Ferguson dropped off? Should he call the man and find out? He decided this might be done, but first he wanted to check out some figures.

The company sold its electronic components directly to factories which, in turn, assembled them into finished electronic equipment for industrial use. An analysis of these figures showed that Ferguson's sales to his larger accounts were down substantially, although his sales to the smaller factories were holding up well. This was puzzling. You would normally think that attention to the larger accounts would be more rewarding to Ferguson, who earned a good proportion of his salary from commissions. The Sales Manager then decided to analyze sales by product group in Ferguson's accounts. The breakdown, shown in Table 3, was revealing.

	Thousands of dollars		Performance
Product Group	Quota	Actual	Actual/Quota
Transistors	$ 70	$ 80	114%
Microwave tubes	150	150	100%
Semiconductors	430	160	37%
Photoelectric cells	100	110	110%
Auxiliary products	50	50	100%
Totals	$800	$550	69%

Obviously Ferguson was having trouble selling semiconductors, normally used in large quantities by his biggest factory accounts. Was this caused by Ferguson or were semiconductor sales beginning to slacken?

Further analysis by product for the entire East Coast indicated that semiconductor sales were beginning to drop off. A competitor had cut prices and was making inroads. What is really significant, however, is that sales for other product groups were high, and this disguised the loss in market share for semiconductor sales.

Because overall company sales were on target, most sales managers would never have bothered with this analysis. They probably would not have traced the problem to Ferguson. The day was saved only because the Sales Manager used his detective instinct. He adamantly refused to accept things at face value. Due to his efforts, an early trend was discovered and a change in the company's marketing tactics allowed it to avert a major loss of sales and profits.

The corporate manager can take full advantage of the detective instinct. By refusing to accept any conclusion until it makes sense he will avoid making major errors. By examining motivation until it thoroughly explains surface moves, he will avoid serious mistakes. By questioning any deviation from expected performance, he can be expected to uncover major changes in the pattern.

Credulousness

Credulousness is not generally regarded as a manager's weakness but I have seen it damage careers many times. Unfortunately, some managers display surprising readiness to believe anything they are told if the statement comes from a source they respect. The dangers here are quite obvious. If a manager, for example, is gullible enough to accept the hasty conclusions of a subordinate, time and money can be wasted, sometimes in prodigious amounts. If he is foolish enough to believe the stirring rhetoric of an unreliable person, he is headed for trouble.

It never hurts to question yourself about a man's motives when he feeds you gratuitous information designed to make you take action. It is also provident to check on results of subordinates, particularly when they have been known to be inaccurate in previous matters. These are not cynical actions. Rather, they characterize the careful manager who understands the importance of making decisions based only on the most reliable information.

In one case, the former Manufacturing Vice-President of a metal fabricating company accepted the cost figures for a new plant as supplied to him by his Director of Manufacturing. The Director assured his boss that the figures had been carefully obtained with the help of cost accountants and project engineers. The Vice-President examined letters supplied by those departments which vouched for the accuracy of the cost estimates.

The Vice-President accepted the cost figures without even a perfunctory check of their accuracy. The cost estimates subsequently turned out to be immoderately low, and the Vice-President lost his job.

Whether or not the Director of Manufacturing deliberately supplied false cost figures is not the point. His boss stupidly accepted the figures without a question. Since this project was a costly undertaking, all hell broke loose once actual costs exceeded estimated costs. And since the Vice-President was the man in charge of the project, he was the guy to get the axe. He should have been more careful.

Too many managers in big jobs display surprising readiness to accept anything they are told. They are taking inordinate risks with their jobs. Prudent managers will take the steps necessary to ensure that any important decisions that are going to have their names attached to them will have only the best chances for survival.

Obtainable Goals

Nothing reveals the immature personality as quickly as the tendency to set up unrealistic goals. The manager who submits a proposal without first having carefully thought through its merits, attainability, and implications no longer deserves to be called a manager. It is commendable to want to cut costs by 30 percent; it is another thing altogether to have the means at your disposal to do so. In the business world generally, and most certainly at the managerial level, there is no room for witless dreamers.

Tragically, many businessmen haven't learned that lesson. Many a company has a large quota of bright young men who are so intent on being regarded as bright that they sponsor only the most dramatic work-improvement programs. Invariably they have found a way to double sales, capture 50 percent more of the market, cut costs in half, or implement a new system which will revolutionize the industry. Even the most cursory examination of these incredible proposals will reveal one or more major faults.

An old Spanish proverb reads: "Goals without means are like bread without flour." This sums up an important test about maturity. In business, a display of this kind of weakness can spell disaster for its sponsor.

Promises, Promises

Have you ever had your boss promise you a raise or promotion and then, probably through no fault of his own, renege on his promise? It just about shrivels the desire to do a good job, doesn't it?

The point here is very simple. Avoid promises like the plague, but if you make one, then for God's sake keep it, regardless of the circumstances! There is nothing that so crushes your peoples' morale as unkept promises.

Promising too much to subordinates to gain their goodwill is a common mistake made by young managers. There is often a strong temptation to hint to subordinates that a comparatively small effort on their part will be substantially rewarded. This temptation must be resisted on all occasions, for when the balloon bursts, the drop in morale will be large indeed. Unfulfilled promises destroy confidence in the boss. From that time on the boss will never be trusted, and this distrust will eventually spread to other members of the staff.

The manager most likely to have the respect and loyalty of his staff is the manager who never makes promises unless he is absolutely certain that he can keep them—and even then he will be careful, because he is mature enough to realize that something unexpected might happen to wreck his chances of delivering.

Managers and Mistresses

Contrary to the accepted corporate folklore, I don't think having a mistress is necessarily detrimental to a manager's career. Social mores, as we all know, have become quite liberal over the last few years. We need only look at the recent crop of films and printed material to verify that. The new books and movies strongly reflect a sexual permissiveness that society would not have condoned just a few short years ago. Although business is regarded as one of the few remaining bastions of conservatism, even here the Victorian outlook is being changed gradually by a more liberal, enlightened management. Nowadays, many businessmen turn their heads the other way when they discover one of their peers is keeping a woman. That in itself, is tacit acknowledgement of its increasing acceptance.

Corporate tongues, however, really start wagging when the manager commits one or more of the following blunders in picking a mistress:

1. When the girl is an employee and quite obviously receives special privileges. The manager who grants too-generous raises to his secretary-mistress deserves to be fired.
2. When she is a married woman. I don't think it's necessary to belabor that point.
3. When it affects the manager's job. The mistress syndrome is undeniably revealed by swollen expense reports, two-hour luncheons and a sharp increase in "sick" days.
4. When the manager starting a relationship with a girl fails to assure himself that he is not taking her away from someone else—like the president of the company. That's the kiss of death.
5. When the girl is not attractive. Think for a moment what your attitude was when you heard that a manager you knew was having an affair with a particularly striking young lady. If you're honest with yourself you suffered a momentary

pang of jealousy which was quickly supplanted with a genuine feeling of admiration for the manager. You probably muttered to yourself, "Lucky stiff." Whether or not you would have liked to have an affair with that same girl—or any other girl—does not matter. What is relevant is your admiration for his prowess with women. On the other hand, you probably felt revulsion for the manager having an affair with a girl acknowledged to be considerably less than attractive. Your opinion of that manager dropped a notch or two.

Every manager has to make his own decisions. If he really wants a mistress then he simply must face up to the possibility of trouble. Although businessmen no longer look down their noses at the manager and his mistress, that relationship is still fraught with risks. Any manager who is serious about his career will probably resist the impulse.

Socializing With Your People

This is one time the litany of management is right. It is sheer folly to socialize with people who report to you. Naturally you will associate with those people you like and that tragic day may come when you must discipline or even fire a close friend. Don't let this happen to you. If you must socialize within the company, select your peers.

A manager can maintain respect for himself only if he does not become unduly intimate with members of his staff. It makes obvious good sense for him to maintain a friendly attitude toward his people and to let them know that he is genuinely interested in their needs as human beings, but he must understand that, as a boss, his first and major consideration is the quality and value of work of his staff. If the manager should ever allow a subordinate to feel that he has a strong claim on his indulgence, sooner or later that employee will create a problem for the manager—very possibly without ever meaning to. Friendliness without intimacy, courtesy and consideration without social obligation—these relationships are necessary to maintain the constructive attitude of his staff.

Zero Defects And Other Slices of Baloney,
or
Achieving Product Quality

Zero Defects is nothing more and nothing less than management's fervent desire to push a button and watch its quality problems disappear instantly. It is wishful thinking at its zenith.

Unfortunately it doesn't really work. Zero Defects means *no* defective products whatsoever. To get workmen to that stage requires first that all raw materials, tooling, and supplies be letter perfect. Then it is possible to help the workmen achieve near-perfection. (*Not* perfection.)

Remember though, that other workmen at supplier's plants make the raw materials, tooling, and supplies. Therefore the supplier's input must also be perfect, and before that is possible, *their* suppliers must provide perfect raw materials, tooling, and supplies—and so on.

After the attractive facade of Zero Defects is torn away, and after the guts of the program are examined in minute detail, it becomes all too apparent that Zero Defects is one step removed from a cleverly promoted gimmick. In the final analysis, quality of product is achieved only when top company management *insists* that its products must be the best on the market. Note that I said *insists*, not *desires*. There's one hell of a difference. When a company's management says it sincerely desires its products to be of top quality, what it's really saying is this: "We've got 100,000 units to produce this month, guys, and ship them we will. Unit cost can't exceed $2.75, and God help the poor bastard who goes over that figure. Oh yeah, I almost forgot. I don't want you guys to ship any junk. Last year our customer warranty figures went through the roof. Let's try to hold it down this year."

Now, when a company *really* means that it wants top quality, it will set quality goals such as maximum warranty costs, number of customer complaints, or any other indicative index. This goal will then be communicated to all members of management, and middle management will be required to formulate a plan which delineates ways and means of achieving product quality. The plan will be executed, and the actual results will be compared periodically to planned results. This feedback from the customer to the company will permit management to assure itself that the quality goals are, in fact, being achieved. And if they are not, management will at least be aware of the problem, and they will be in a good position to correct discrepancies.

Management goals are best achieved when numerical goals are established and followed. Quantity of sales, costs, production—all of these are quantified. Quality can be measured that way, also. When it is, it becomes comparatively easy for management to measure its progress.

One thing for sure: Zero Defects, quality posters, quality campaigns, and quality programs will never become usable substitutes for measurable quality goals. Rather, they can (and do) become ways and means to avoid squarely confronting the issue of obtaining quality goals.

Part Two
CIRCUMVENTING CORPORATE POLITICS

People are not always what they seem.

Gotthold Lessing
NATHAN der WEISE, Act. 1, Sc. 3

Knowing how to 'look good' is just as vital to the executive as doing a competent job. But to know how to 'look good' first demands that the executive shed any illusions he may have about ethics and morality in the business world.

A noted management writer

When I showed the manuscript of this book to a young supervisor who had recently graduated from college, I was not prepared for his reaction.

"I enjoyed the book", he told me, "but I would argue against your Part Two, "Circumventing Corporate Politics". This section spoiled everything for me. Nobody would ever believe those things really happen in business. Why don't you leave out that part, and just stick to the truth?"

As I told the young man, every line of this book is true, and one of the unfortunate realities of business life is corporate politics, like it or not. Anyone who holds the illusion that his company is different, that his management won't permit infighting, that politics do not exist—anyone so naive will never become a success in the corporate environment. He will be knifed and knifed hard before he reaches the next rung on the corporate ladder.

It's a tragedy that businessmen cannot concentrate their entire efforts on just doing a good job. Unfortunately, that isn't enough. Office politics *do* exist—and they exist *everywhere*. Aspiring businessmen will learn how to do their jobs well, but just as importantly, they will learn how to protect themselves from the vicious thrusts of corporate knife artists. They will recognize that no Geneva Convention exists to outlaw executive warfare. They know that attacks on their positions may come from their peers, their juniors, or their seniors. They recognize that the cost of defeat is the loss of livelihood, even though it may be concealed by the polite phrase, "voluntary resignation."

Politics are inevitable wherever people work together. This section is devoted to building the protective armor of managers who accept that fact. It characterizes the typical moves of corporate politicians and infighters. The first article sets the stage by disclosing the real meaning of business ethics. Subsequent articles develop the corporate-politics theme on a personalized basis.

One last word before you read Part Two. You have available one very effective weapon for self-defense: your ability to recognize things the way they are, coupled with the ability to remain icy calm and objective. If you can master the art of seeing things exactly as they are, you'll probably survive all political attacks and emerge as a toughened, disciplined, and outstanding executive.

Ethics in Business?

The litany of management would have you believe that there are ethics in business. The idea makes for good public relations, but if you buy it you stand a fair chance of being taken to the cleaners—and businessmen in a position to evaluate your potential will be highly disappointed in your naiveté.

True, the management litany is inundated with high-sounding appeals which create the illusion that management is guided by the very same ethics applicable to private life. Articles on ethics in business appear regularly in the management journals and periodicals, claiming that ethical behavior is a sound, profitable aspect of business life.

Their authors are not being fully honest with you. You've got to read between the lines. What they are really saying is that in the long run a company can only get itself in trouble if it antagonizes the general public and squeezes the customer too hard.

Now please do yourself a favor and do *not* shrug off these words as the discontented rumblings of a cynic. I am being very honest with you. After many years in business one thing is very obvious to me: The closer you get to the core of business, the clearer it is that the businessman's ethics are often just a thin veneer covering the hard realities of life.

Actually, business does have a code of its own. It's a quite workable code, too, but it is completely pragmatic and should never be confused with what we loosely term "ethics." Often younger, relatively inexperienced businessmen get the two confused. I once attended a company meeting that was called to discuss the repercussions of approaching federal regulation within its industry. The keynote address was made by a young man who proudly recited how his end of the operation was preparing a self-policing set of regulations for the company's plants. Radiating conviction and enthusiasm, he was like a zealous missionary attempting to convert the hopeless natives.

After this fiery address, the company's plant and regional managers assembled privately to discuss the effect of the proposed federal standards. No one present could doubt their common attitude. To these men, the self-policing regulations were designed to prevent the Federal Government from imposing stern restrictions on the company. In other words, those regulations were conceived as protection for the company, not only the public—and nobody at this meeting deceived themselves for one moment about its purpose.

If you give this some hard thought you will understand their conclusion. We live in a society governed largely by the rules of private enterprise. The government imposes certain restrictions on business to prevent excesses of competition. Within the framework of these requirements a company is free to do everything it sees fit to do, regardless of the "ethics" involved—provided, of course, that the public isn't hurt or deprived. If the company's actions fail to meet with the public's approval, then sales and profits will fall and the company will be penalized. This is the great regulator of business and it describes the business code.

Another generally misunderstood aspect of the business code is the relationship that exists between companies and their salaried employees. On any given day in the American business world untold numbers of businessmen are being fired, demoted, or placed on innocuous jobs. (This last category is sometimes called "special assignment.") Frequently these decisions are questioned by company employees and outsiders. It is hard to understand why a manager with 30 years of experience is suddenly forced to the sidelines; or why a promising young executive who has made substantial contributions to his company finds himself in the unemployment office on Monday morning.

These are natural questions that many management writers have discussed in print, and to people not privy to corporate decisions, the seemingly arbitrary removal of talented and loyal men is puzzling. It cannot be argued that many firings and demotions are inequitable and arbitrary. Capable managers are removed, for example, to make room for the boss' relatives. Also, many good men find themselves out on the street because of mergers and consolidations. There are any number of unfair reasons that can be and have been used to remove managers.*

Yet, the lion's share of removals reflects the dynamic business code of American business in action. Companies *must* make a profit to survive. And to make a profit, companies need men who can do the job. If managers are unable to produce and are incapable of holding up their end of the business, they must then step down and let others take over who can do the job. It's the ability to be effective that normally defines the boundaries of success or failure on the job. I say "normally" for a reason; there have been and will continue to be cases in which capable managers are removed from jobs simply because the jobs themselves have been eliminated. This does not reflect negatively on the managers; if they are good men, chances are their companies will find challenging positions for them in other areas.

How, then, is loyalty rewarded? Is it fair to demote a man who has given selflessly of himself for 30 years? By the public's concept of ethics the answer is NO. In the public's mind the demotion would represent a flagrant injustice to the employee. But this is confusing the business code with ethics, and they are not the same. From any company's viewpoint, keeping a man on the job demands that he be competent. If he is not, the entire organization—whether a handful or thousands of people—is in danger. Because of one incompetent performer, many may fall. Parameters of the business code for employees are shaped by performance; by the rules of the business code, nonperformance means failure and removal. Nonperformance, in fact, is equated to the business code much in the same way that sin is related to religion. Both are transgressions.

---

*I am ignoring business layoffs due to general economic conditions, which is a subject in itself.

Sizing Up the Cutthroat, or Guerilla Warfare

You have just become manager of your department, but already somebody is after your job. The bigger your job in the company hierarchy, the more certain it is that you'll have to fight for it. Don't delude yourself that your company is above office politics. It isn't. Wherever people are working together and where personal gain is tied to personal recognition, you'll find politics. That's everywhere; business, government, academe, everywhere.

You have the prerogative of blithely ignoring this fact of life and proceeding happily on your way. (If you do, you'll never make it to the executive suite.) Or you can learn about politics and thrive within the system. You needn't become a knife artist, a cutthroat, but to be successful demands that you do learn to recognize the cutthroat and understand his modus operandi.

These are some of his typical moves:

He may be your peer. Since you are new on the job he will simulate friendliness, aiming at your naivete and inviting you to lunch. You feel gratified that you're making new friends in the organization. Your guard is down. If he's learned that the boss stresses attendance at monthly staff meetings, he will say: "I'm going to miss the monthly meeting next week. I like to attend them but the boss doesn't care if you go or not. It's mostly a formality anyhow. He doesn't attend himself half the time."

Just a few words, mentioned casually. Then the cutthroat moves on to another subject. You can bet *he'll* be at the next staff meeting, but if you're gullible enough to swallow his story and not show up, then you may hurt your reputation with the boss.

Perhaps you're both trying for a higher-level job. The cutthroat, who has eyes and ears everywhere, has been told that management wants someone who will take over smoothly and keep things the way they are. Out of feigned goodwill he takes you aside and says: "I just got the word on the opening. They want someone dynamic to move things around, get everybody out of a rut; someone who can make things happen. I'm going after this job with everything I've got, and I know you are too. Naturally, I hope I win, but if I don't I'll never hold it against you. Good luck." He then shakes your hand.

Again, his apparent honesty makes you drop your guard. You feel a developing sense of camaraderie. Here is a guy, you think, who will be your friend, come what may. You go for the interview and follow his suggestion.

"You know the department," the V.P. says to you. "How would you handle it if you get the job?"

"I'd probably reorganize it," you reply. "While I have a lot of respect for the fellow who ran it, I think many things would have to be changed; organization, product line, and work methods to name just a few."

The V.P. looks at you, blinks his eyes a few times, and suddenly you get a queasy feeling at the pit of your stomach. You have been had—and now, irrevocably, you're out of the running. Next day your "buddy" is interviewed, says the right things, and gets the job.

Suppose you're a Regional Manager of Sales. Market Research has uncovered a major shift in demand for your products. Unfortunately, the Manager of Market Research wants your job and deliberately keeps this information from you. Other managers are told verbally about the development but you are kept in the dark. Later, sales begin to drop off in your region, and the V.P. of Sales is breathing down your back. You say you are not aware of the reason and the V.P. blows his cool. "How the hell," he says, "could you be unaware of the shift in product demand? For Christ's sake, everyone else knew about it."

You are shocked to hear this information. You maintain that you were not told by Market Research. But you're on the defensive now, and the M.R. Manager has moved one step ahead. He insists that he told you, and because he told everyone else, they all—including your boss, the v.p.—think you've started to slip. You've had it.

The cutthroat has his own creed, diametrically opposed to every decent impulse and tailored to take advantage of such impulses in others. It goes something like this:

1. Never consider the feelings of other people in the business world, but be sure to give the appearance of doing so.
2. Hard work is commendable—other people's. (The cutthroat believes in the Horatio Alger slogans, provided someone else does the work.)
3. Appear to respect others—if they believe you, they are more easily manipulated.
4. The team approach is important—it enables you to blame others for your mistakes.

5. Never step on your friends—unless you have to.
6. It is kindly to hold on to failures—they can be controlled and used.
7. Sex is fun—particularly if you get to the boss' secretary.
8. Above all, never do *anything* without a purpose.

Infighting

Competition among peers is desirable in business. It stimulates performance and encourages members of the organization to strive for recognition. But when competition becomes destructive, when one man is deliberately pitted against another, then the company and the men involved will be hurt instead of benefited. Violent rivalries develop, job performance is seriously impaired, and good men leave the company.

You would think that serious managers recognize the impact of this basic truth. They don't. Internal harmony is the exception rather than the rule. As a management consultant I have visited many companies and the infighting I have seen in some of them has made me seriously wonder how the hell they ever got anything done.

When I start an assignment with a client company, relations among managers normally look good. But when I begin talking with members of the organization over a two-martini lunch, the facade is discarded. The combination of booze and the knowledge that management consultants hold their silence (a consultant who can't isn't going to be a consultant very long) is just the opportunity a man needs to open the floodgates and spew out the venom that has been building up in him for a long time. Now I discover that half the company's managers are engaged in life-and-death struggles, the atmosphere is drenched in suspicion and mutual distrust. Resumes are kept up-to-date just in case. Able men are gunning for the jobs of other able men. Managers become too preoccupied with self-defense, and the quality of the work begins slipping.

The most saddening part is that infighting isn't necessary; it can be held to a minimum, if not entirely abolished. Members of the organization could pool their efforts and work in cooperation to achieve company goals. Moreover, infighting is *not* a necessary concomitant of business. Neither is it usually launched by business rivals or peers.

Almost always, it starts at the top. The boss encourages it; he wants it that way; he thinks he can get the best from his staff through rivalry instead of through mutual interest and cooperation. The idea is that each man will do his utmost only if he is fully aware that he is being stacked up against somebody else.

Unfortunately, it doesn't work that way. The competitive instinct invariably turns against the other man rather than being channeled to the work at hand. The infighting begins.

I recall one situation vividly. In the Slitting Department of a southern aluminum fabrication plant Mr. Jackson was promoted to General Foreman. This was a new position in the department which had been specifically created to tackle its increasing production problems. The Department Manager, to whom Jackson reported, was Mr. Robinson, an old-time employee with the company.

Jackson was a young, aggressive engineer, well-trained in production and cost reduction techniques. He attacked the department's problems systematically and soon most of them were eliminated. He improved production output, reduced operating costs, and mastered several of the department's quality problems. Within a short period of time the department was running at peak efficiency.

That's when Jackson's problems started, not ended. His boss, Mr. Robinson, began running scared. He had managed the Slitting Department for six years, and had never achieved in that entire period what Jackson had accomplished within ten months. Robinson became increasingly anxious about holding this job. He had three years to go to retirement, but he felt that Jackson was a real threat to him; a threat that could cost him his job.

As Department Manager, Robinson could have been considerable help to Jackson. He had over 30 years in the business and there was very little about aluminum fabrication he did not know. If his extensive experience could have been coupled with Jackson's youth and fervor, the combination might have been unbeatable. But his energy and drive had withered away several years ago, and his only goal now was retirement. He not only did not want to help Jackson, but he wouldn't even if he was forced to. All he desired was to hold onto his job for three more years.

Robinson used every conceivable opportunity to tell his boss, Mr. Franks, the Plant Superintendant, how he was solving the department's problems. Actually, Jackson was the person responsible for obtaining results, but Robinson attempted to get the credit himself. When Mr. Franks would ask him about Jackson, the reply would usually go like this: "Well, he's okay, Mr. Franks, a good boy. I know he's trying to do the best job he can. Someday he's going to make it, too. He's a little light in experience, but time will cure that. I'm bringing him along as fast as I can."

It wasn't long, however, before Jackson caught on to what was happening. He, in turn, would casually attempt to talk with Mr. Franks whenever he could. During these conversations he would imply that Robinson was delaying progress of his several projects and not contributing to the department at all.

Before long Jackson and Robinson were at each other's throats. Each man spent more and more of his time plotting against the other and the situation began deteriorating rapidly. It didn't take too long for production to begin slipping and costs to begin rising.

At the same time the feud had reached its peak, my company was hired to make a cost analysis in this plant. Since I had had several years aluminum experience I was one of the consultants assigned to the job. When I started I was pleasantly surprised to discover that Mr. Franks and I were alumni of the same college.

When you're a management consultant you learn to take advantage of coincidences. It wasn't long before we became friends. One evening, after work, we decided to have a few drinks and during the course of the evening we progressed to the stage of exchanging small confidences. It was then that I was told about Jackson and Robinson.

I listened carefully to the story and then asked Mr. Franks how he intended to handle the situation. He looked at me intently, took a long pull on his drink, and said: "Smitty, you're a nice young guy, but I'm going to tell you something. There are times you have to keep your fingers out of the pot, and this is one of them. I don't have the slightest intention of doing anything. Listen, Jackson and Robinson don't fool me for one minute. I've got both of them pegged. The've been trying to shoot each other down ever since I had Jackson promoted. But I promoted Jackson for a good reason. Not one goddam single solitary thing was getting done. Robinson's been on his ass now for too long, and I had to get things moving again."

"Why don't you simply replace Robinson with Jackson?" I asked.

"I can't. Robinson has three more years until retirement, and I can't fire a man with his length of service. Jackson's a good man, a real competitor. Robinson's no slouch in that respect either. I figured if I threw them in the pit together and let them fight it out, Robinson may quit or opt for early retirement. Either way, I get what I need out of this. Production costs are down, although not as low as I want them to be. I don't give a good goddam if they strangle each other."

This utterly cynical approach is obviously devoid of any real understanding of human nature. While Mr. Franks was quietly watching from the sidelines, those two men were tearing at each other's jugulars. Two formerly healthy management men had become anxiety-ridden ghouls, so preoccupied with defending their own hides that they could no longer be effective on the job.

Infighting is tantamount to corporate suicide. The knowledgeable manager can easily foster an atmosphere of mutual cooperation, replacing the deadly battle of wits that can be so detrimental to company profits. But first he must recognize the signs of infighting. They probably exist in your own company now. These are the symptoms to watch for:

1. Each of the two men constantly seeks the approval of the boss—more than should ordinarily be expected.
2. Each creates opportunities to criticize the work of the other.
3. Interoffice memos start flying.
4. The work begins to slip.
5. Each man casts aspersions on the other man's abilities.
6. Each man becomes excessively tense and irritable.

If you observe any of these signs among your staff, get your staff together and tell them, in no uncertain terms, that you will not tolerate their interference with job performance. Let them know their personal antagonisms must take a back seat to individual accomplishment. You won't eliminate their antagonism to each other by doing this, but you will severely diminish the destructive infighting. It won't surface if they are aware that you know about their feud, and are determined to stop it. The manager who creates a good working team is ten steps ahead of the one who creates strife.

Compatibility with the Boss

Do not delude yourself that relations with your boss are founded entirely on your job competence and success. You must be a contributor, but that in itself will not necessarily endear you to the boss. The relationship is more complex. You can possess every conceivable positive attribute and still not make a good showing at evaluation time if your boss really doesn't like or trust you.

Every boss has one or two key subordinates. These men know how to heighten the boss' effectiveness and sense of well-being. They are men who can be trusted without limitation and they will not usurp authority. In effect, they have adopted the boss' value system. They are shrewd enough to have asked themselves: Does the boss want an easy-going, slow-moving second man, or is he tough enough to demand an aggressive assistant? Then they mold themselves according to the boss' preference.

Hypocritical? It depends on your viewpoint. Some people would undoubtedly sneer at another's attempt to pattern himself on what the boss likes in his men. But their disdain does not change that fact of life. The manager interested in assuring himself the best possible chance for success must be flexible enough to adapt to the way things are, and not wait for the way he would prefer them to be.

I know a man who was appointed Director of Engineering in a small company. He was a tough and demanding executive, probably aggressive to a fault. The Vice-President of Engineering who hired him was a decent but cautious man. Both men appeared to complement each other nicely; the director was fast-moving and resourceful while his boss was thoughtful and deliberate. It looked like a winning combination.

After the Director had been on the job six months he was fired. Being an intelligent man, it didn't take him long to reconstruct his mistakes. As he later confided in me, he had unwittingly

been ignoring the boss by demonstrations of his independence. He had seldom consulted with his superior before making decisions on major projects. Against his boss' wishes he had instituted several minor changes in the organization. In almost every respect he had been doing too many things too fast to please the boss. He learned too late the necessity of establishing his personal compatibility with the boss.

If I could record the impressions and reactions of readers of this article at this very moment I am sure that many would be mentally sneering and thinking: "Boy, is this guy way off base. With that kind of attitude I wouldn't know how he gets *anything* done at all."

To those readers I would say: Don't write off my words so quickly. Forget your subjective judgment, and take a moment to view this subject coolly, dispassionately. Ask yourself: "What's the best way to get the boss to buy my ideas?" This question will steer you away from any subjective and emotional reactions. It will force you to concentrate objectively on the issues and to analyze the available options. The answer should be obvious: *The manager who can get his ideas most readily approved is the manager who is accepted by his boss. His position is vastly superior to his peers who have not pleased the boss. The boss will not give their ideas the same consideration.*

Now guess who's going to get the most done in your department. Guess who will then be afforded the most recognition in terms of advancement opportunities, raises, bonuses, and stock options.

Don't get the wrong impression. I am not advocating that a manager become an obsequious yes man. Far from it. Any manager worth his salt who disagrees with his boss is obliged to state his concern and the reasons supporting that concern. But he should concentrate on facts and issues rather than relegating his interest to which person is right in the discussion that he has with the boss. Any fool can satisfy his ego by telling the boss he is wrong. But the intelligent manager can get his point across by squarely confronting the issues and avoiding any "ego" confrontation with the boss. That accomplishes nothing.

How about the manager who steadfastly refuses to adopt or even accept the boss' point of view? He may feel egotistically superior to you, but he is less a man than you are. Why? Because he has allowed his emotions to displace his objective determination to get a job done. He has permitted the word "achievement" to take a back seat to the word "pride." Pride is just another fancy name for ego, and ego has been one of the most prevalent reasons for destroyed careers. The manager who allows his ego to dominate his life is a manager who fails his company and his boss, but mostly himself.

On the other hand, the manager who has his boss' ear is the man who can put his ideas to work. He is the achiever, and in the final analysis, he is the manager who makes things happen.

Angels

An angel is a management man going places or one who has already arrived. The ambitious junior will try to hitch his wagon to the angel's star in hope of moving along the same upward path. When a boss on the move is promoted, he is likely to take with him his most useful and loyal subjects (if only for self-protection), even though they may be less competent than other available men who are not as well known to him. This is known as having an angel or sponsor.

As an example, the Vice-President for Marketing of a pharmaceutical firm moved to another company in the same industry, only this time as Executive Vice-President of Operations. He took with him his Manager of Training who, with the new company, became Director of Personnel. Within two years the Executive Vice-President moved up to President of the company and his Director of Personnel became Vice-President of Personnel. Nice movement for an individual only two years removed from middle management ranks. His angel was soaring.

Besides the obvious benefits of upward mobility associated with angels, there is another powerful benefit that the manager can take full advantage of. Other people are made aware of the closeness between the manager and his angel. If the angel is in top management, all the better. The manager's bets or tactics will always be taken seriously. Even when he is suspected of bluffing, his rivals will hesitate to challenge him. His personal influence is felt everywhere, and other management men will listen carefully to his ideas and proposals.

A manager in this position will be smart to make his influence felt in only the most constructive and positive manner. Rather than ignoring or insulting others he will go out of his way to create a congenial atmosphere while showing his respect for others. If he doesn't, and if someday his angel is removed from power, then the enemies he has made over the years will dive on him like a pack of vultures and rip him to shreds.

Beating the God-Players,
or
Dehumanizing Management Through Personality Tests

Indicate whether you agree, disagree, or are uncertain.
1. I am going to hell.
2. I often get pink spots all over.
3. The sex act is repulsive.
4. I like strong-minded women.
5. Strange voices speak to me.
6. My father is a tyrant.

Questions such as those shown above were originally a by-product of efforts to screen mentally disturbed people; they measure degrees of neurotic tendency and were meant primarily for use in mental institutions and psychiatric clinics. If they sound familiar to you, don't worry. You haven't gone off the deep end—you've just been screened for a manager's job in industry.

Psychological testing has its place in our society, but that place is not in the halls of corporate management. Psychological testers claim to eliminate "unacceptable" candidates for employment, and I suppose that sometimes they do. But any manager can tell you that now and then the lemons still slip by. However, that's not the most important criticism. Far more important is the fact that while the psychological testers are eliminating the unacceptable job candidates, they do so at the incalculable cost of eliminating with them any number of highly qualified men who would be tremendous assets to the companies whose testers reject them. And since very few executives are trained in psychology, they accept what the psychological testers tell them and never know what potentially valuable manpower they are turning away.

The fact that many questions asked in psychological tests are humiliating and dehumanizing is bad enough, but what's worse is that psychological testing is accepted in hundreds of businesses throughout the country, and any manager who changes jobs can expect to run afoul of it sooner or later—probably sooner. The only thing you can do is to learn to beat the testers at their own game.

It can be done—if you'll follow a couple of simple rules: First, never, never underrate the cleverness of the psychological testers and their tests. Second, learn what they consider safe and acceptable answers—and always give them. If necessary, lie without hesitation. As an aid to understanding and passing psychological tests, let me recommend Martin L. Gross' *The Brain Watchers* (New York, Random House, 1962). This is an excellent book, and any normally intelligent manager who studies it will greatly increase his chances of getting by the psychological testers.

Personally, I've been through the psychological testing routine about two dozen times; I'm a scarred and weary veteran of personality and ink-blot battles. Yet I have learned not only how to cheat (yes, cheat) on the tests, but also how to hold up under the intense pressure of a two-hour in-depth interview with a clinical psychologist.

It wasn't always that way. During my earlier experiences with the testers I was naively unaware that the best answers to the questions on personality tests should always indicate a conventional, run-of-the-mill, pedestrian personality. I didn't realize that you were an "immature" manager if you:

a) Liked books and music.
b) Placed family before job.
c) Loved your mother just as much as your father. (If you were reared in a fatherless home, you'll *never* pass the personality tests, unless you cheat like hell!)
d) Did things differently.

Let me cite an example about doing things differently. Several years ago I was interviewing with a large international company located in New York. The position, which was in the Corporate Industrial Engineering Department, had a lot of top-management visibility and I was eager to get it. I knew intuitively that they liked me and respected what I had accomplished for my previous employer. Only one obstacle remained: to pass the company's personality tests.

I made an appointment with their clinical psychologists and subsequently endured the long, grueling tests which, as I recall, lasted about six hours. They threw everything at me. Since I had recently completed *The Brain Watchers*, and since I had faithfully applied what I had learned, I knew that I had done well on the tests.

So far, so good.

Finally, for the last hour or so of the day I was scheduled for an in-depth interview with one of their resident psychologists. The interview actually went superbly. Applying my knowledge once more, I was able to field all his questions and pryings and realized that I was on my way to becoming a new member of their management team. But the psychological testers never let up (you must always remember that), and this one was no exception.

During the final 15 minutes, and seemingly as an afterthought on his part, he smilingly said that he had only one other little thing he wanted me to do—write a one-paragraph story about my home life.

I don't need to tell you I was well prepared for that one. In fact, I had been half expecting it. But I was off my guard. Feeling that I had already won the war I quickly began writing my story.

Honest to God, his eyes started to bug out and he shot a long thin finger accusingly at the paper in front of me.

"You're printing, you're not writing. I told you to write a story."

I couldn't believe it. I tried to recover: "I always print. When I had mechanical drawing in college I was trained to print, and I guess it's habit now."

He picked up the paper and examined it closely. And then he smiled and concluded the interview.

One week later I received a letter from their Personnel Department which said the job had been filled by another applicant. They needn't have bothered writing.

I was very disappointed. I thought, however, that I could salvage something from the experience, so I called the Employment Manager and pressed him to find out the psychologist's findings. Because the manager was basically an honest, straightforward guy, and since he didn't have to put it in writing and commit himself, he told me. It seems that the psychologist had decided that printing rather than writing expressed a sense of inferiority, a lack of desire to move ahead and to commit myself to courses of action. Since the job I had applied for demanded a man of commitment, I was dropped like a burning charcoal at a picnic.

Enough said. Since then I've learned never, never to drop my guard with the God-players. Now I stay on my toes right up to the last menacing second.

And you can do it, too.

Meeting Style for the Careful Manager, or POOP

Every living creature has its own natural habitat; mountain goats scamper around the rocky sides of high mountains, birds flock south every winter, alligators lurk in warm swamplands, and corporate phonies thrive at meetings.

The Phenomena of Ossified Phonies (POOP) can be observed and studied almost everywhere across this great land of ours. From the highest councils to the lowliest assemblies, at least one and usually several phonies are ineluctably in attendance. Their presence, however, can be detected only by the most careful observation, for these fellows are clever creatures indeed. The novice, attending his first corporate meeting, is completely unequipped to distinguish between the contributor and the phony, and it is to this poor soul that I direct the following guided tour.

The Meeting Place

The phony always seeks to hold the meeting in his office rather than somewhere else. This, to him, is a status symbol. He feels very superior when his colleagues come to his lair. Thinly disguised by an air of magnanimity, the phony maneuvers and struggles so that he can preside over meetings, particularly those attended by his peers.

Size of the Meeting

If the phony has anything worthwhile to say (which is seldom) he invites as many people as possible. Whether or not those invited have anything to contribute is immaterial. What matters is that the greatest possible number of people be there to be impressed by his sage advice and masterly command of the situation.

Words, Words, Words

If the phony has nothing worthwhile to contribute (which is most of the time) he can always deliver a ringing, extemporaneous speech on the subject at hand. Although he is saying absolutely nothing, the conviction in his resonant voice and the determination in his eyes convinces everyone present that here is a man both knowledgeable about the problem and doggedly resolved to do something about it.

Conviction

The phony always blows with the strongest wind, but he never, never gives that impression. His nose is keenly attuned to the shifting wind and he staunchly defends whatever view prevails. The careful observer can detect the phony's oscillating viewpoint by watching him nod assent to conflicting arguments presented. The more important the speaker, the longer and harder the phony's nod.

Making a Decision

We all recognize the nature of meetings. There is little danger of *any* decision being reached. Nevertheless, if that memorable occasion should ever occur, the phony won't be involved. There's never an adequate reason for him to abandon his amateur standing. Of course, if the decision is a unanimous one, he may attempt to take credit for it, provided it's a sure thing.

Leaving Meetings

The phony is a master escape artist. If conditions get heated during the meeting, he will suddenly look at his watch and exclaim: "My God. I'm late for Mr. Anderson's meeting." The phony has scored two points. He automatically makes his getaway without arousing suspicion, and since Mr. Anderson is a vice-president, he has chalked up another one on his peers. (Whether or not he is going to Mr. Anderson's meeting is entirely irrelevant.) He then hastens to the cafeteria for coffee and a roll, sighing with relief.

Conference Style

The way a manager handles himself during conferences determines, to a large degree, the reputation he has with his peers, boss, and subordinates. His chances of gaining influence among his associates may be weighted by their impression of him during meetings. It is, therefore, quite important that the right things be done. The astute manager can help himself considerably by adhering to the following "rules" which have been developed by executives who understand the importance of conference style.

1. *Never Be Competitive in a Meeting*
    Don't attack the other man even though you know his idea is ridiculous. Sit back and let somebody else shoot him down or let the idea die by its own weight. Don't criticize what he says, and if you have a better proposal, word it in such a way as to allow the other man to save face. Why make enemies needlessly? If you're a manager the chances are that you have your own detractors; It's foolish to add to them. Besides, if you attack someone else, other conference members will think you a fool. They'll lose respect for you.
2. *Keep Your Viewpoint Consistent*
    Nothing exposes the amateur as quickly as shifting viewpoints. If you take a stand on an issue and then suddenly reverse course—even though the change may be entirely justified—you run the risk of having it rumored that you crumpled under fire. Whether you like it or not, consistency in the conference room is regarded by others as a sign of strength. The best way to handle a change of viewpoints is outside the conference room, in private conversations. By letting others believe that your further investigation of the matter has caused you to alter your course, you will gain a reputation for being open-minded.
3. *Always Take the Positive View*
    Never be *against* something; rather, be for the opposing viewpoint. Stress the positive approach. Taking a stand against

something gives others the impression that you are negative and against progress. If you can't think of any positive way to support the opposing view, then hold your fire.

4. *When Attacked, Remain Cool*
You may be seething inside when you're openly criticized in a meeting, but if you show it other people may think there's something in the criticism. Never say to a man who is attacking you, "You're wrong." Try something like this, instead: "I see what you're talking about, Paul, but there are some facts you may not be aware of. Once you see the whole picture, I think you might change your mind." Now you've put Paul on the defensive. You have hinted that he may have spoken without sufficient preparation. Another important step has been taken: you have relegated the issue to facts, not opinions. If Paul fails to cooperate with you now, he will appear to be subjective and hostile. In contrast, you stand out as an objective manager who has only the best interests of the company at heart.

How Not to Write Memos

First, it is important to realize that memos should replace dialogue with your staff and other members of the organization wherever possible. This will not only bog down and confuse communication within the firm, but it will also give you the opportunity to hire another luscious secretary to keep up with the typing backlog. Keeping this point well in mind I have devised the following guidelines to immortalize the writer of memos. Always remember that:

1. The primary object of the memo is to impress the people who read it. The memo need be only incidently concerned with the subject at hand.
2. Limited distribution of memos is the indisputable sign of a miserly person. Spread copies of the memo freely, regardless of interest on part of the receivers. *Always* include the Board of Directors.
3. The standard rules of being concise, meaningful and interesting definitely go out the window. A long, detailed, and rambling memo gives the impression of bulk and thought. People will think the writer scholarly.
4. You should never come straight to the point. That is a sure sign of an immature personality.
5. It is an act of kindness not to send the addressee his copy. This will save him the embarrassment of knowing that top management has read a memo critical of his department.
6. You never list names of receivers in alphabetical order. Start with the person considered to be the most influential and list the other names in descending order of importance. This will provide an excellent opportunity to "stick it" to one of your peers. Always list this guy's name last, after the janitor.
7. Any ideas developed by your staff should be included in the memo—provided you get the credit. There is one time-tested way to accomplish that. Do not write: "John Jones,

my staff assistant, has developed a method to cut costs." Write: "My department has developed a method of cutting costs." The latter statement has the unique quality of a double-edged sword. First, of course, management will most certainly be impressed with the aggressiveness of your department (which, in their minds, is you). Second, they will think you modest for stating "My department," rather than "My idea." Without doubt you will not only receive the credit personally, but top management will consider you a man of great humility for not mentioning that it was your idea.

Skirmishing Tactics

The Litany of Management advocates only direct and straightforward encounters in the everyday business world. Granted, the manager should achieve his goals by the direct approach most of the time, particularly if he is to gain a reputation for being fair and honest and above-board.

There are times, however, when the direct approach isn't effective. This is notably true when the manager is dealing with people who aren't honest. In those cases a flanking movement is sometimes more rewarding than a direct assault. And there are those situations in which the manager feels it important to conceal his motives for other reasons. Typical skirmishing tactics, as they may be called, are described in the following subsections.

Table the motion

One of the most effective methods known for killing a project or a proposal is to delay it. Nothing cools the ardor of proposers and supporters of unwanted ideas so much as time. In parliamentary parlance, it is politely referred to as "Tabling the Motion," and nowhere is it used more profusely and professionally than in our U.S. Congress. How many times have you heard of a tabled motion from a congressional committee sputtering into life again and becoming a law? Seldom. A proposal tabled and delayed until a subsequent congressional session usually is forgotten quickly, and sometimes gratefully.

I once had a boss who used this tactic on me (I recognized the stall but too late to counter it). I wanted to bring into my department—on a lateral transfer—a young, ambitious engineer who worked in another department of the same company.

My boss was opposed to the move, but he didn't tell me that. He disliked the young man involved and knew that if he voiced his opposition directly he would encounter stiff resistance from me. Instead he suggested that it was wrong to move a supervisor to another area without promoting him. Because there were no higher-level openings at the time in my department, my boss recommended that we wait until a suitable vacancy occurred.

I had been finessed perfectly. His argument was above reproach and I could do nothing about it. Of course, I realized it might be a year or two before the right opening occurred, and by then the man would probably be somewhere else, unavailable. My boss knew that too, and he was counting on it, and the tactic was effective from his viewpoint.

Call the bluff

Ordinarily, calling somebody's bluff should be avoided (it puts him in a corner, and if you are wrong you're going to look awfully silly), but sometimes the tactic is beneficial, at least in the right circumstances. Here's an example:

A manager I knew couldn't resist the temptation to tell everybody at weekly staff meetings just how wonderful he was. At one of these meetings the problem of inadequate merit increases for first-line supervisors was being discussed. This manager imperiously stated that if something wasn't done about it, then he would personally confront the Vice-President in charge of Personnel and state his case in no uncertain terms. At this juncture his boss whipped out his appointment calendar, and with a straight face said, "Damn good idea, Jim. When would you like to see him? I'll have my secretary set up the appointment."

That stopped the manager cold. He knew—and his boss knew—what the consequences would be. If he dared to go over the head of his boss's boss (the Vice-President of Manufacturing), his career was finished. Well, he wasn't about to do that; his bluff had been called, and he folded as quickly as a tire going flat.

But the point had been made—either he put up or shut up. Not too surprisingly, he was very careful about what he said from that time on.

Use the grapevine

A top quality supervisor who worked for me had a real problem. He was one of those people who was five minutes late to work every morning. It didn't make any difference what time his shift started, he would invariably be late. If starting time was 7:00 a.m., he'd come in at 7:05. If it was 8:00 a.m., he'd be right there—at 8:05.

This guy was a damn fine producer, and he commanded the respect of all those around him. So I wanted to get my message across, but I wanted to give him the opportunity first to correct his fault without my having to tell him.

How did I accomplish that? I used the grapevine. I had my secretary pass the word along that I was getting very much concerned about tardiness, and I was contemplating the use of strict regulation and policing to enforce the rule. The word was passed along, and the supervisor eventually heard it. Since he didn't want any blemishes on his record, he soon learned how to better plan his time, and the fault was corrected. That saved him the embarrassment of having to be corrected by his boss.

Stay behind the scenes

There will be times when it's necessary for you to appear to support a plan of action when in reality you are opposed to it. For one reason or another open opposition to the plan is not wise, organizationally. You might even have to give your consent to the plan, but with secret intentions to kill it somehow.

For example, an ambitious contemporary might propose a new departmental procedure. You are quite aware that the procedure is ineffective, but someone in top management thinks it's the greatest thing since x-rated films. Your only alternative is to openly support the idea while looking for ways to sabotage it. You might suggest, for example, that Cost Accounting generate a cost-savings analysis for the plan. Because you already know that the procedure's cost will outweigh its savings potential, you are fully aware that Accounting will squash the proposal.

If you think this move cynical, you're wrong. You are doing what you know is best for the company, but in such a way as to avoid becoming the scapegoat. It wasn't a workable proposal anyway.

Conceal your interests

Along the same line of thought, it never pays to blurt out your true desires and interests while bargaining.

Suppose you want to cut department costs by $20,000, and you know that in a section managed by one of your subordinates it would be possible to eliminate two jobs that would accomplish that goal without harm to the section. If you disclose this to your subordinate, you have weakened your bargaining power considerably. Knowing your strong desire, the subordinate may bargain for a raise as payment for the cost reduction.

It might be a better tactic to tell your subordinate that costs are out of line in his section, and that it would be to his advantage to cut them by $20,000. Tell him that failure to do so will make his section look bad in the eyes of management and that Accounting will highlight the high-cost area until the cost reduction is made. If your man is halfway worth his salt, he will know that the two people he has been holding in reserve will have to come out of the budget.

You have then put the responsibility in his hands—where it should be—and protected your bargaining position.

Commit it to writing

If the subordinate tells you that he is unable to reduce costs by $20,000, ask him to put it on paper. The very act of writing down his inability to do what is expected of him will force him to reconsider his position. Surely it will make him think through the alternatives. He realizes the memo will not make him look good in the eyes of management.

As a general rule, asking that something be committed to writing is a sound move. Sometimes it will generate a 100 percent about-face, and your objectives will be accomplished.

Swatting Flies

Every manager must understand that his critics and adversaries will mount frequent and annoying attacks on his flanks. These minor assaults are not serious enough to sabotage the manager's work, but they are often irritating enough to divert his efforts momentarily while he shakes them off.

Taking the time to shake off such harassment can sometimes be a mistake. The manager must learn first to distinguish between the infrequent but serious attacks on his efforts and the many but insignificant swipes against him. By necessity, he must divide his time between defending his flanks from the serious attacks and pushing on to successful culmination of his plans—and that leaves precious little time for handling skirmishes. A manager, in other words, does not have too much time to swat flies. He cannot permit himself to be deterred by minor assaults and some of the petty kind of infighting so common in corporate halls today.

Under such circumstances, his best tactic is to see no evil and hear no evil. The manager must concentrate on those goals he wishes to achieve and brush aside the irrelevant but annoying assaults of his adversaries.

This tactic, the avoidance of swatting flies, is most particularly applicable to the successful handling of trivial irritations. The manager who devotes his time to answering petty criticisms does not look good in the eyes of either his subordinates or his superiors. He appears to be a man easily distracted from his goals. The best way is to ignore the flies pointedly as if they were inconsequential. This makes the manager look more mature than his adversaries, and people will gain respect for him. It is one time when it pays to be "above it all."

Part Three
HANDLING CORPORATE PERSONALITIES

Jesus, there are so many different types of people, that I get all confused when I try to handle each of them.

A new manager in industry

By itself, circumventing the intricate web of corporate politics is not enough to assure success on the job. Technical competence and administrative skill are additional prerequisites. And then, of course, the adroit manager must understand how different personalities can affect his work. These personalities can be broadly categorized into such types as do-gooders, purists, and numbers men. Politics aside, the typical corporate personalities will have a great effect on the manager's career—particularly if he isn't capable of first recognizing and subsequently handling the moves of these people.

The various operating methods of corporate personalities are explained on the following pages. No attempt has been made to list all types—that task would appear to be endless. Rather, some very typical examples have been selected, which, if carefully studied, will provide clues for identifying other personality types the manager will encounter in his working day.

Corporate Do-Gooders

The most dangerous threat to business is not lurking on the far left; nor is it to be found with pressure groups attempting to legislate quality into consumer products. It has nothing to do with hippies or militant organizations.

The most dangerous threat to business is the Do-Gooder. This insidious monster takes the form of an honest, sincerely motivated management man—who has no idea just what the hell kind of havoc he is creating in the organization. Neither is he aware of what he is doing most of the time. The Do-Gooder's trademark is his ability to somehow manage to do the wrong thing while making it appear temporarily to be right. He doesn't act through malice; on the contrary, he is genuinely interested in doing right by himself, his department, and his company. The Do-Gooder is a dedicated man.

He is also a threat to his company and to all those unfortunate managers and supervisors who tie their wagon to his deceptively bright star. The Do-Gooder is a loser.

Whatever he sets his hand to ends in abysmal failure—but seldom for the Do-Gooder himself. Somehow, he miraculously escapes too-close association with the sinking ship, while some poor boob who's been responsible for just part of the project catches pure hell for a botched job.

In his own mind the Do-Gooder can do no wrong. He honestly believes that what he is doing can only benefit the company. This rigid belief in self is charismatic. He radiates such confidence that normally intelligent people become thoroughly disarmed and are attracted to his projects. They are hypnotized by the deceptive aura of success surrounding him and volunteer their services to the cause. Sensing a winner, they climb aboard the bandwagon. Without realizing it, these unsuspecting boobs are in for the ride of their lives. The road ahead is full of washouts, but all they can see is the open highway.

Let's watch the Do-Gooder in action.

First he must get an idea. Normally it will not be his own, but once he finds one to his liking he attaches himself to it like a leech. In the case I have in mind, the Do-Gooder, a marketing manager whom we shall call Dick, got an idea from a company salesman which entailed a radical change in the company's method of packaging one of its products. Without investigating the feasibility of manufacturing the new package, Dick made a presentation to the company's marketing board. With the zeal typical of an evangelist he sold the concept for the packaging change to the board.

Armed with the marketing board's approval of the idea, Dick composed a fiery, imaginative letter outlining the new packaging concept and shot it off in all directions within the company. Anybody remotely concerned with the project received a copy of the memo. In it, Dick lauded the idea and hinted at immortality for those fortunate few wise enough to hop aboard early and contribute to the project's success. It was really a magnificent sales pitch.

WARNING 1: *Be wary of flowery-worded, high sounding appeals. Remember, a soldier (manager) can die (lose his job) for the cause.*

A mass meeting was called at which Dick exhibited the same charismatic fervor that he had with the marketing board. The idea was instantly accepted by most of the managers at the meeting. Plans were undertaken to make experimental and pilot-plant tryouts*. Research and product managers enthusiastically suggested several potential methods of successfully manufacturing the new package. Almost everybody was carried away by the project. A few cool heads, however, visualized innumerable difficulties. These men understood Dick's idea; they basically agreed with the concept and realized the benefits that would accrue to the company should the new package become a reality. They were also painfully aware that chances for success of the project were slim. They recognized that the new packaging con-

---

*A pilot-plant tryout involves transformation of a new product from the laboratory experimental stage to full conditions of mass production.

cept required an entirely new technology—one that the company, having neither the money nor the expertise, could not provide. These few men did not voice their doubts. Instead, they remained silent.

WARNING 2: *If you are one of the cool ones, and you recognize a half-assed idea when you see it, hold your tongue. Even though you are firmly convinced that the idea is goofy, you dare not say it. You will be accused of being negative.*

Elaborate preparations began immediately, and soon a few dozen of the new packages had been produced in an experimental laboratory under closely controlled conditions. Dick was ebullient. He circulated a memo, profusely thanking research and engineering for their rapid development of the process. In the memo, copies of which were sent to the marketing board, he forecast glorious sales estimates on the basis of the research manager's optimism about his success in the laboratory. Next, Dick requested that advertising and sales promotion develop a way to merchandise the product. According to him, the project was ready to move into the manufacturing pilot-plant stage.

WARNING 3: *There is a vast difference between manufacturing a new product under laboratory conditions and manufacturing it under mass production conditions. The success of the former is not related at all to the success of the latter. Any manager who predicts success of a project on the basis of a small-sample, laboratory-controlled experiment without a tryout in production doesn't deserve the title of manager. He is about to get reamed.*

The entire project fell apart in the production pilot plant. There, thousands of packages were needed to verify the process, rather than the few produced during the experimental phase. The huge amount of time and attention devoted to the new package in the laboratory could not possibly be duplicated under production conditions. There just wasn't that kind of time and money available. Within the first week of the pilot-plant run it became abundantly clear that the new package could not meet the cost, production, and quality standards that the company considered necessary for one of its products. The entire project was scrapped.

The inevitable post-mortem analysis started. Every manager even remotely associated with the project sweated out the possibility of being singled out for blame. When a great deal of money is thrown down the drain, some poor bastard takes the brunt. That's as inevitable in business as federal taxes. Total costs of the project amounted to $45,000—all wasted. Dick, our Do-Gooder, did not feel the tiniest pang of remorse. In his own mind, he was completely blameless. The stupid research manager, who had so foolheartedly expressed his unbounded optimism, took the ride. He didn't lose his job, but higher management pegged him as a boob. Boobs do not make vice-president; neither do they receive adequate compensation. They just hang on to what they have—and pray.

Dick's reputation remained unscathed. To this very day he roams corporate halls, looking for just that one idea that will take his company (and him) to the top of the heap. His path is strewn with the wrecked careers of many unsuspecting and gullible managers.

WARNING 4: *Learn to spot the corporate Do-Gooder. Once you know him stay the hell away from him. Do not become associated with his projects. He is more potentially destructive than a commando team.*

Purists at Work

Every organization has its purists. The larger the company, the more it has. A purist, or nit-picker if you will, is that person who concentrates his efforts on minor and trivial details. He is unable or unwilling to take on the more significant and meaningful aspects of his job—those tasks that produce results. The purist is an insecure person who lacks the ability to get things done. He is often aware of this shortcoming and thinks he can make up for it by attacking procedural details.

The purist is characterized by indecisiveness. If he is in a position of responsibility, he's a menace when the chips are down. Almost all of the bottlenecks in his department are caused by his deliberate avoidance of problems. He will hesitate on projects and objectives for so long that nothing gets done. Any work done by his subordinates is delayed while the purist nit-picks minor details of the subordinate's work. Invariably, at rating time, the purist finds many things wrong with his people and their ratings reflect his insecurity. He is a buck-passer and an object of derision among his subordinates and his peers. He is that type of person who wants a recommendation from a committee before he'll decide, and even then his decision will be delayed.

If you should ever be in the position where you find yourself working for a purist, then get out of his organization as quickly as possible. Don't make the mistake of trying to outlive him on the job. It's very possible that it will take management a long time to catch up with him. In the meantime he will be attributing lack of results to *you*, and he will be telling his boss just that. If his boss hasn't yet determined the root cause of failure (the purist), you could easily shoulder the blame until he does. It can irreparably damage your career.

What happens if you find yourself working for a purist but for one reason or another, cannot quickly get out of his organizational area? How do you manage to live with him?

You will never come to any good working for a purist, but here are a few guidelines to help ease the pain and maintain as stable a relationship as possible under the circumstances.

1. Never threaten his position, either by words or by action. Remember, he is a terribly insecure person, and at the slightest provocation he will accuse you of being uncooperative and consider you a menace.
2. Forget achievement. The purist will hold up your project as long as he can, particularly if it is a good piece of work. This will cause you no end of frustration, but don't yield to it. Rather, expect it to happen.
3. Keep a record of all ideas, suggestions and proposals made. The purist will forestall their acceptance, but you may be able to use them sometime in the future when you are working for someone else.
4. Keep within accepted boundaries. Carefully follow every established protocol and procedure. Regulations must be your bible because the purist knows no other way.

Numbers Men,
or
Don't Fall Prey to the Statisticians

In almost any occupation, any discipline, you will find people who will try to impress you with a dazzling combination of fancy reports and unintelligible technical jargon, confident that you are not familiar with their technical speciality. In too many instances their work will not stand careful scrutiny. Too often they are masters of theory who are either unable or unwilling to apply their craft to the hard realities of increasing sales or cutting costs.

Numbers men can be found almost anywhere, in any occupation. The density of numbers men, however, is proportional to the increasing complexity of their specialities. There will be found, for example, fewer numbers men in production than in accounting, and fewer numbers men in accounting than in statistics.

Ah. Statisticians. Let's pause for a moment and examine these prime examples of what is meant by "numbers men." Many of the statisticians I have known in management appear to be governed by Parkinson's Law of Triviality. Briefly stated, this law means that time spent on any project will be in inverse proportion to its significance. While the company is being eaten alive by soaring production costs, its statisticians might be blithely figuring ways to add another useless computer or two to the business. (In a company I worked for, the statistician recommended replacement of the company's time-sharing terminals. His reason: The newer terminals did not clack as loudly as the old terminals. They were quieter. So help me, it's true.) Conversely, if the company is momentarily successful its statisticians will not request a mere computer or two. No. They will appeal to management for a new computer complex along with a multitude of new statisticians and technicians (see "Weeding

Out Bureaucracy and Deadwood" on page 6). The exact purpose of the complex may be obscured by statistical jargon, but the desire for it is unmistakable.

Never worry, though; there can be a happy ending for management. Simply keep decisions on such matters at the highest level—even the decision to change the time-sharing terminals or to add one statistician, particularly the latter. The climate upstairs will be ruthlessly hard-nosed about the practicality of every expenditure. It's hard to get a worthless expenditure past the controller. Put the decision in his hands.

If you're about to work on a particular project with the company statistician, then heed this warning: Statisticians may have a grasp of the numbers, but many of them are unable to interpret the numbers properly. Let me give you one example:

My company was developing a new product. We were concluding the experimental stage and were ready for a production try-out. Because the product was new and because machinery and tooling had to be modified and operators trained to handle the new process, we had decided on testing larger-than-normal samples at each stage of the process. This is a routine and prudent move. To assure the reliability of the sample we requested the company statistician to develop a dependable sampling plan for us. The entire project was carefully explained to him since we wanted him to be aware of every conceivable point that could affect his results.

The project was ready for the production tryout four weeks later. Unfortunately, the statistician had not yet developed his sampling plan, and our timetable accordingly was set back ten days while we anxiously awaited the birth of his masterpiece.

The baby was born all right, but it had no arms, no legs, no head. The statistician had played it exactly by the book. For every 1000 pieces produced he suggested that we test 110. Since the test involved was destructive, this meant destroying 11 percent of everything produced. The statistician vehemently defended his proposal, claiming that it had come right out of his statistical manuals. Maybe it had, but our accountant verified that destruction of 110 pieces would cost more than production of the entire 1000. Statistical manual or no, that would have run us right out of business.

Possibly because of rigid academic training, possibly for other unknown reasons, many statisticians are not properly equipped to fuse the theoretical with the pragmatic into workable results. Of the many statisticians I have encountered during my business career, only a handful were capable of translating theory into practical results. Accordingly, I would not recommend their employment in any management-related position unless their abilities were first carefully scrutinized.

In much the same manner, managers must beware of numbers men in all areas of business. While they may understand their figures, they rarely understand the significance of those figures to the business operation. They are to be avoided, for not only will they fail to make solid contributions, but they may also cause needless and costly delays in progress.

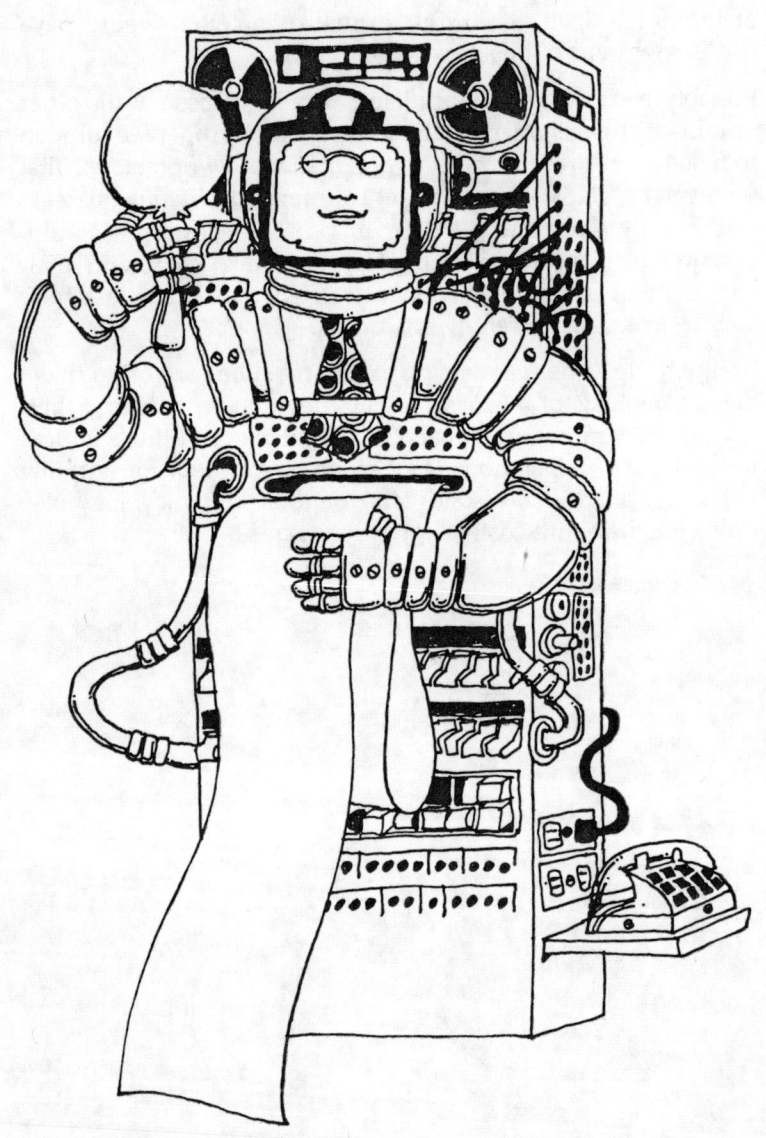

High Priests of the Computer Room

One of these days, and I don't think it's too far away, somebody is going to catch up with the high priests of the computer room. For years the systems men have been enjoying what amounts to a privileged sanctuary in much the same way that diplomats enjoy diplomatic immunity to the laws of the country in which they are serving. It is only to be expected that the mystique surrounding the computer cult will be torn away, probably by financial vice-presidents who have heard all they want to hear from their high priests. The systems men have for too long used the apparent complexity of their trade to hide from the very unpleasant necessity of justifying their existence.

Let's take a first step here and strip some of their gears:

1. Computers are just manufactured pieces of equipment that are programmed to do certain things, just like machines that are built for the factory. Contrary to accepted belief they haven't been imbued with the power to reason. They just go clickety-clack.

2. Systems men are enveloping their jobs with a cloak of mystery, and they have no more right to do that than the engineer who designed the machine for the factory. Systems men must be trained to concentrate on profitability and service in much the same manner as other staff men.

3. All computer systems must be evaluated for profit contribution, and once the systems are operating they should be examined periodically to assure their continuing profitable use in the organization.

4. Now for the most important point. The manager of the systems department should *not* be a person immersed in systems technology. Rather, he should be selected from outside that area—a reputable person who has done a good job in a department as far removed from computers as possible. The point here is that the outsider can appraise each of the systems department's activities without being blinded by the technical

expertise of the systems men themselves. His lack of intimate knowledge about computer systems almost guarantees the resulting lack of sympathy for nonprofitable "works of art."

Unfortunately, a positive realignment of the systems men's profit attitude isn't always enough. Too many other members of the management team are fervent believers in the computer cult. For it is here, among people unfamiliar with systems, that computers can easily become ends in themselves, rather than means to an end. It is in production, marketing, engineering, and research (technical groups primarily) that management people fall in love with the apparent sophistication of the computer, and common sense evaporates as quickly as sprinkles of rain on a sidewalk on a hot summer's day.

This attitude, devoid of common sense, is puzzling. Why, one could ask, are management men, trained in the concepts of profitability and service, so vulnerable when they deal with computers and systems? What unknown factor causes them to shed their highly developed "results-getting" orientation and succumb to the rather common mania of "computeritis"?

The answer is a subtle one, indeed. Technical people are particularly sensitive to criticisms about failure to keep up with the latest technical developments. There is a pervasive urgency to be familiar with and to use the most up-to-date concepts in the field. The more technical the staff work, the more urgent the pressures. That is why love affairs with computers, for example, are more common among research scientists than among production engineers. Both groups, however, are vulnerable. The difference is only a matter of degree.

Using the newest technology is not a bad thing. In fact, it's sometimes a competitive necessity to advance the state of the art and make substantial contributions to company efforts. The shortcomings are not associated with technology itself, but with the people using it. Their motivation is often questionable. Is the newly designed $50,000 computer research program aimed at developing a new product for the company? Or is it being used solely to enrich the ego and satiate the curiosity of the research scientist who instituted it? In too many instances it is the latter case.

There are no easy answers to the problem. As long as there are technical people, and as long as there are advances in technology, there will be a strong tendency to use the latest thing. But the wise management team can take full advantage of that. It can consider the new technology, allowing the technical man to express his beliefs about its applications through a well-defined feasibility analysis. It can ask such questions as: Will the new technology help establish a new product or improve an existing product? Will it enrich profits? Will it contribute to sales? Will it provide information to help advance management's knowledge in a particular area?

The use of directed yet flexible thinking applied to the latest in technological developments is a sure cure for "computeritis."

Craftsmen can be Costly

There are craftsmen working in specialty groups who, unknowingly, generate untold dollar losses because of their compulsion to make a product or perform a service on a level which greatly exceeds the company's specified quality requirements. These people mean well, but they can create terrific headaches for their managers. Craftsmen until their dying breath, they would never dream of doing less than an excellent job on any assignment.

For example, look at the industrial chemist who orders only the finest grade of chemicals for a particular application for which lesser grades, cheaper in price, would do as well; or the tool and die maker who insists on imparting a mirror finish on a stamping die when no finish at all is specified on the blueprint; or the design engineer who specifies tolerances of millionths of an inch when only ten-thousandths of an inch are needed.

These people are craftsmen of the first degree, but they are creating needless expense—and by doing so they are making their managers look bad through high cost reports. This type of expense can be minimized when the problem is recognized and intelligent controls are maintained over the work of the craftsmen involved.

Where is the manager most liable to find these craftsmen? In what occupations are they likely to be concentrated? Generally, the more complex and skilled the work, the greater the tendency of the craftsmen to seek perfection. Using a crude index based on the factors of skill and complexity of work, it is easy to visualize craftsmanship categories as shown at the top of the facing page.

Obviously, if you manage a tool and die shop or a research foundation you will want to be more aware of the craftsmanship phenomenon than if you manage a production operation employing unskilled people. However, the index is *only* a

Level of craftsmanship	Examples
Top	Tool and die maker
	Design engineer
	Research scientist
High	Electrician
	Pipefitter
	Production engineer
	Bench chemist
Average	Semiskilled occupations
	Unskilled occupations

generalization. Likely as not, the craftsmanship urge or desire for perfection will be found among some members in semi- and unskilled occupations, while some of the more specialized occupations will have members who are interested in average work only.

Craftsmen aren't necessarily confined to the sciences or crafts; they can also be found within the management profession. Visualize, if you will, an accountant stubbornly hanging onto reports containing vital information for management until their punctuation has been verified; or the quality control supervisor steadfastly refusing to approve manufactured parts until they have been inspected for the third time. Granted, some of this is generated by insecure or defensive personalities. Much of it, however, can be traced to the craftsmanship urge.

Management itself can occasionally create a craftsmanship problem. A perfectionist boss can drive his employees to protect themselves by producing at quality levels far—and wastefully—above specifications. Every manager, therefore, must know precisely what his department's quality requirements are—and adhere to them.

Managers confronted by the problems attributable to corporate craftsmanship can lessen its impact through intelligently applied controls. For example, a machine-shop manager began an inspection of all finished work for workmanship defects. This inspection revealed that too many machinists were putting out too many jobs of a quality far exceeding company specifications. Use of this information permitted the manager to work with the craftsmen involved and explain to them the cost of perfection. Soon, the quality of the work performed stabilized at a level above specifications, but not so far above them as to generate undue cost. Controls of this nature and the sensitive interpretation of them have helped curb the phenomenon of corporate craftsmanship.

The Cluttered Desk Phony

Many people will argue with this, but I think that a cluttered desk indicates that something's wrong. I've had that point brought home to me time after time. Let me give you an example. I once called on a design engineering executive in my capacity as a consultant. The great man left me cooling my heels for almost an hour in his reception room. When he finally deigned to admit me to his office (the supreme accolade; I should have been overjoyed), I noticed that his desk was piled high with mounds of paper: letters, blueprints, catalogs, memos, specifications, along with a variety of paperwork I couldn't even begin to identify. All of this paper was strewn about his desk in aimless fashion.

As I sat there, basking in the great man's presence, he was interrupted frequently by a number of telephone calls. I took that opportunity to more closely examine some of the papers on his desk. Much of the correspondence was from three to six months old, and in the middle of one heap of paper was a dog-eared copy of Playboy magazine. It wasn't much later, after some months on my consulting assignment, that I became familiar with the executive, and I learned that his apparently slothful habits were attributable to his fear and insecurity. He was using his desk as a filing cabinet to look busy, praying that his minor deception would not be uncovered.

A variant of that occurs when the occupant is deliberately putting on a show, not necessarily because of a feeling of insecurity, but to impress other people. Unable to do a job, this phony attempts to deceive others with an apparently work-laden desk. This virtuoso performance can be shattered easily by close examination of the papers on his desk. In almost all cases, very few of the papers will be current. An abundance of old and obsolete reports will be evident. Flush this phony out by hiding (or better, destroying) all the papers on his desk. Without his shield he'll be as embarrassed as a monk at a nude encounter group.

In one respect or another, a cluttered desk is a manifestation of poor working habits. It is important to remember that sloppy work habits breed sloppy thinking, and sloppy thinking usually results in sub-par work.

The Research Man Syndrome

The battle between management and research is unending. Management wants "directed" research while scientists want "pure" research. Management expects its research people to be company-oriented while scientists work *in* an organization rather than *for* it. Management demands profit-and-loss accountability while scientists couldn't care less about these mundane matters.

Succinctly, this is the root of the problem: The management man is confusing the role of the company scientist with his own. The management man thinks in terms of sales, profits, effectiveness, efficiency, and handling people—and he unconsciously assumes that the same organizational orientation can, and should, be attributed to the scientist.

He is wrong.

These things are completely irrelevant to the typical research man, who perceives his role in the company as that of an unshackled innovator. This the management man cannot understand. To him, the job of professional management is paramount, and he sees it as a necessary segment of each and every division of the company, research included.

This reaction is to be expected. Naturally, management tries to adjust the scientist to the organization rather than the organization to the scientist. With mediocre performers it can do just that and still have a harmonious group. But it cannot do so with the brilliant research men; only freedom will make them harmonious.

But even those scientists who are considered mediocre seldom achieve the insights credited to their counterparts in management. Purpose is anathema to the scientist. His every impulse directs him to research that is *not* directed. Planning, systematized development, achievement geared to profits: all of these are foreign concepts to the scientist, and he impatiently brushes them aside to work on those projects that satisfy his curiosity.

The more successful research organizations are not necessarily the ones that operate within the framework of established management concepts. The more successful research organizations are the ones that produce new products, more versatile raw materials, and improved manufacturing processes. If you had the opportunity to study such an organization, you might be amazed to discover that many of its people are *terrible* managers, handling budgets, plans, quantitative yardsticks, and similar management accouterments in a vague and uneasy manner. The organization's scientists are more concerned with experimentation. Even if the experimentation is part of a directed research effort, the scientist is more at home and happier in the laboratory than he is in the office, where such pressing concerns as scheduling, workload planning, and people problems must be handled on a daily basis.

The successful research organization, then, has harnessed the efforts of scientific research without imposing the yoke of profitability and efficiency on its scientists. Those important matters are handled only by top research management working in conjunction with the controller's office. Administrative matters are taken out of the scientists' hands almost entirely. They are given a broad set of goals toward which to work. Progress is checked periodically by research managers. If individual performance appears lackluster, then the research managers are responsible for correcting each situation. In no case, however, are the stringent workloads assumed by other segments of the company imposed on the research scientist. The result, in most cases, would be a notable lack of contribution. Scientists do not respond to the same stimuli as managers.

The controlling factor is decided by the amount of money that management is willing to invest in research before obtaining its stated return on investment. For example, if a research organization, composed of two hundred scientists and technicians, costs the company five percent of sales, and this organization goes two or three years without introducing any major new development, some drastic and sudden changes are indicated to bring that department back in line with company goals.* Conversely, the same organization which successfully develops a significant new product every year or two would probably be judged successful. It all depends on management's definition of expected return on investment for the research dollar.

An astute management will not use the same criteria to measure success for its research organization that it uses to measure other divisions of the company. Rather, it will recognize the climate needed to develop new products and, within reason, will grant research people a measure of freedom greater than that experienced in other areas of the company. This climate will be maintained at the level necessary for the company to realize its desired return on investment. New products, new processes, and new materials are mandatory to allow the company to remain a viable entity in the marketplace. As long as a steady flow of new developments is forthcoming, the research team is doing the job management is paying it to do.

---

*I arbitrarily selected five percent of sales for an example only. The actual figure depends on company goals, desire for new products, and a host of other factors.

Secretaries

A few thoughts on your secretary. It is important that she be pleasant and get along well with people. A grouchy and irritable secretary reflects negatively on her boss. Picture, if you will, your boss' opinion of you if your secretary is permitted to cat-fight with his secretary. If your gal happens to be one of those snarling creatures, get rid of her—fast.

Another thing. Don't allow your secretary to become overprotective. When she starts to screen your telephone calls and your visitors, the time has come for you to put your foot down. Regardless of how she feels, her judgment cannot be substituted for yours. Managers have enough artificial barriers surrounding them without creating any additional ones themselves.

When you start working together, get your relationship with her established early. By nothing more than the tone of your voice or the look in your eye, you can draw a line between you and your secretary which must not be crossed. That line, unstated but very real, must establish a business relationship between you, nothing more. Your secretary must realize that she is your employee, not your social acquaintance, however friendly you may be. She is working for you in a business enterprise, not a social situation.

If you're lucky, you'll get one of those girls that not only can use her head but wants to. To a secretary of this caliber, application of her secretarial skills may not be enough of a challenge. Let her decide which letters to answer and, if she's capable and experienced enough, what to say. Develop her into a real assistant by delegating work that will relieve your burden while satisfying her desire to be creative.

Part Four
DEBUNKING ACCEPTED PERSONNEL THEORIES

The blunt fact is that we are a long way from realizing the potential represented by the human resources we now recruit into industry.

Douglas McGregor
The Human Side of Enterprise, p. vi

There's nothing fundamentally wrong with our country except that the leaders of all our major organizations are operating on the wrong assumptions.

Robert Townsend
Up The Organization, p. 137

The propagation of the Litany of Management is the responsibility of the corporate personnel department.* For it is usually from most personnel departments that the Litany flows. Personnel policy, management development, training courses—all of these and more make the Litany a living, viable, persuasive philosophy. Managers in the corporation structure have the responsibility of applying this personnel policy as successfully as possible within their organizations.

Personnel men are the missionaries of the Litany of Management. Their job is to bring "the word" to the natives. "The word," as we are discovering, is the golden set of rules that managements use to keep their people in line. Loyalty, honesty, hard work, strict adherence to company policy, etc. are typical phrases and words from the gospel. Not all of these are bad, of course, but for many of them their basic purpose is restrictive rather than emancipative. They seek to contain and harness the human element unthinkingly to corporate objectives.

The manager who desires to be touched by success must learn to handle the Litany properly. He must learn to sort the effective policies from the ineffective policies. He must be able to manipulate those variables under his control within the framework of personnel policy—without succumbing to the litany. In short, he must learn to survive and grow.

This section identifies some of the more common folktales the manager will encounter in his dealings with personnel policy. A basic understanding of them will enhance his ability to deal effectively with personnel departments and their policy.

---

*Sometimes called Industrial Relations, Human Resources, Organizational Development, Management Training, etc.

People and Personnel

The voluminous texts on personnel theories would have you believe that the motivations and responses of people can be neatly categorized and pigeonholed. From the loins of that brazen assumption a legion of hard-core rules has been spawned which has ruined many a businessman's career. Let's probe objectively some of the more prevalent and treasured theories and see how they fall apart at the seams.

Before we start, however, let's make one general observation. Whenever we discuss people, let's call them people, not personnel. The word "personnel" conjures up thoughts of mechanical precision and infallibility, both of which are more properly associated with machines, not people. Personnel departments (there we go again; it should be "people departments") are racing to keep pace with the scientific age, and the word "personnel," in their way of thinking, has a more sophisticated and scientific ring than just plain "people." People, however, aren't scientific instruments. If we call them by any other name, it is too easy to forget that.

Compromise

The management writers would have you believe that great management advances have been made because management men have had the good sense to compromise on important corporate issues.

Bullshit.

The important advances in management have occurred because a few gutsy bastards have had their way entirely. Theodore Vail was such a man. One of the least-known—but one of the greatest—American businessmen, Vail was president of the Bell Telephone System from just before 1910 till the mid-twenties. His farsighted management decisions, and his resolute determination to allow no compromise to water them down, helped build his company into the largest private business in the world. One of these decisions will illustrate the point.

Vail saw early that his company would have to do something distinctive to retain private ownership. The telephone systems of Europe were being run by individual governments without major problems, and it was just a matter of time before the American government imposed strict controls and regulations or took over the telephone system entirely. To attempt to keep Bell private by publicly defending it against government takeover would be a delaying action only. A policy was needed that would make Bell represent the public interest more effectively than any government agency could.

Vail realized that a nationwide communications monopoly such as Bell could never be completely free of government controls. He decided that the way to minimize government interference was to support public regulation, which, in his mind, was the lesser of the two evils. His stalwart advocacy of this policy met with the stiffest resistance from Bell management and from industry leaders generally. During this period of America's history, public regulation was both slight and ineffectual, and powerful business opposition, aided by the courts, had successfully contained the influence of government.

But Vail knew that it was just a matter of time before the government seized the initiative in regulating private enterprise. Somewhat more farsighted than his contemporaries in industry, Vail recognized that public regulation was vital to Bell's preservation, and he won his fight because he refused to compromise his stand. Due to his efforts, the communication industry today remains within the realm of private enterprise.

There are literally thousands of other examples portraying men who would not compromise their judgments, and because of whom great advances have been made in American business. Read the biographies of Alfred Sloan, Henry Ford, and Robert Wood Johnson, for example. Their success in building huge and vital American businesses was due to their personal vision and their determination to allow no compromise to interfere with the attainment of their goals.

The middle or lower manager today is in a somewhat different position from the pioneers just mentioned. Today's manager must be adroit in his handling of people. He must practice compromise to some extent, but not as much as you may think. It's one thing to handle the boss carefully; it's another thing entirely to put every strength and resource behind an idea or philosophy and push it for all it's worth. Today's manager is hemmed in by corporate policy and regulation. He is surrounded by hundreds, sometimes thousands, of people all united under one corporate banner; people whom he can't afford to antagonize lest he be branded as uncooperative. So compromise in today's corporate environment is a necessity; there's hardly room to avoid it.

But for the manager to make his mark on the organization, he must be a doer. This is a paradox. While he must make his peace with the large number of people he works with, he must also get the job done. To do this demands that he concentrate his strengths and forces on his goals until they are achieved. If in the process he rubs some people the wrong way, then he must decide whether the antagonism of these people is an acceptable price for the achievement of his goals. He must weigh the relative advantages of achievement versus compromise.

It is not an easy task. Being effective on the job is the natural enemy of compromise. However, if the manager desires recognition through achievement, he must occasionally step on some toes. This is a decision each manager has to make himself. It is innundated with risk—but risk is the omnipresent companion of the manager. Whatever the case, do not pay heed to the Litany of Management. If you compromise consistently, nothing will get done. And you will be the loser.

Workloads

According to the Litany, equitable and reasonable workloads should be established for these people in supervisory positions who report to you. At first glance this sounds so plausible that you may never give it another thought.

Please do.

People do their best when they are responding to challenges. Tight, demanding workloads—provided that they are aimed at sound objectives—bring out the best creative instincts in people. Give your people loose workloads or, conversely, unlimited funds, and they will *not* do the best job possible. Without the challenge of tight workloads they will not stir their imaginations to produce those ideas needed by the organization to make it successful. Under pressure, however, your people will discard all the unnecessary and complex work methods. By necessity, they will simplify and aim more directly at the goals. Without doubt they'll moan and groan and bitch—but you can bet they'll get the job done. And what's more, they'll get it done faster and better than if they had been allowed the luxury of less demanding workloads.

Performers

One of the most devastating inferences in the conventional management wisdom is that a top performer can be used interchangeably within the organization. This implies that a good production man can utilize his talents at a comparable job in a staff area or that a good supervisor will make a good manager.

If you believe this garbage you could be jeopardizing your career.

Most people do some jobs superbly but other jobs poorly. The job of the manager is to identify his people's strengths and use these strengths most effectively. Time after time I have watched good men taken from positions they can handle and be placed in jobs they were not suited for—all because some managers mistakenly adhere to the concept that good men are good at all things.

One particular case comes to mind. In the Quality Control department of an equipment manufacturer, a supervisor was promoted to Quality Control Manager. As a supervisor he had had four group leaders reporting to him with a force of about 100 inspectors. He did an outstanding job directing and controlling the efforts of the inspection force. His skill in handling people could only be described as masterly.

Yet the job of Quality Control Manager demanded other attributes of leadership. Besides being technically knowledgeable, the manager had to understand other functions: industrial engineering, production control, customer service, and marketing, for example. The supervisor did not have this understanding and his job performance soon began slipping. While he was capable of managing an inspection force, he lacked the necessary depth and breadth of outlook that the next step up required. He was soon demoted.

Molding People

The supervisor just described might still have been promoted to Quality Control Manager even if higher management had recognized his limitations beforehand. Many times people are promoted in such circumstances because higher management believes men can be "molded" into dynamic performers. Management training courses do much to propagate this fallacy. In fact, however, people are what they are, and nothing more. By the time a man has embarked on his business career, his strengths, weaknesses, abilities, likes, and dislikes have all been largely developed, and his future successes depend mainly on his ability (or luck) in finding those jobs in which his particular background will be appropriate. Any attempt on the part of management to "mold" a person to fit a given job is futile. If the man is qualified to fit the position he will succeed; if he isn't qualified, all the training courses and counseling sessions available will not change his basic make-up—he will probably fail. Management often has too great a tendency to play God in these situations, when actually, it can do the organization no good, besides hurting the man himself. A man is what he is; the astute manager will recognize that fact and use the man where he can contribute most to the organization.

Constructive Criticism

Let's be honest with each other. There is no such animal as "constructive criticism". There is only criticism, period. If you wrap a $300 tailor-made suit around a country boy, you've got a country boy wearing a $300 tailor-made suit. You haven't changed the contents, just the package. The same with criticism. Regardless of how it's presented, it's still criticism, and it must be handled with the utmost care. But let's never fool ourselves into believing that it's anything else.

Is criticism necessary? Yes, but under only two conditions. The first condition is that the criticism be directed toward a correctable fault. It's asinine to criticize a man for something he is powerless to change. If you condemn a weak man for his lack of aggressiveness, the results will be entirely negative. You're not only wasting your time but you're also needlessly damaging the man's ego. The second condition is that criticism should only be directed at correctable weaknesses that are substantially detracting from a man's performance. It would be sheer stupidity to chew out your top performer because he wears wrinkled clothes, but it would be sensible to prescribe a course in accounting to a supervisor who can improve his job performance with a knowledge of budgeting.

How should criticism be given? These are a few commonsense rules:

1. Stress the positive aspect. For example, don't tell the man that his knowledge of some part of the job is faulty. Rather, schedule him for a development course, as would be done with the supervisor deficient in budgeting practices. Sell the man on the fact that knowledge of that subject will enhance his chances for success on the job.
2. Concentrate on performance instead of subjective characteristics and personality traits.
3. Point to the criticism indirectly. Tell the man about similar mistakes you made in the past and describe how you corrected them.
4. Pick the best time, such as directly after the man has received a merit increase. Your recognition of his abilities, as evidenced by the raise, will make the criticism more palatable.

The private life of Henry Jones

Poor Henry. His boss is one of those so-called amateur psychologists, a well-meaning but stupid slob who is sticking his fat nose into Henry's private affairs. Yes, Henry has a problem. His production has dropped, he's been reporting late to work, and he's been seen daydreaming on the job. Something is bothering poor Henry, and his boss is determined to get to the root of it. The boss has just completed a training course in employee counseling and he's just itching to psychoanalyze poor Henry, his first guinea pig.

The boss starts digging into Henry's private life, convinced that he'll discover the reason for Henry's problem. With evangelistic fervor, he peeks and pries until poor Henry is ready to climb the walls. Soon the inevitable explosion occurs. Henry can take no more. With explosive fury he tells the boss to stick the job up his ass, and then flies out of the office. So much for good intentions.

Good common sense advises that a supervisor stay out—way out—of his employees' personal affairs. What happens off the job is none of his business. When a man's performance starts to slip, it's the supervisor's job to bring the man back into line—but not at the expense of the man's pride and dignity. Too-close association of a supervisor with his people's personal problems causes the supervisor to lose his objectivity. And that's the quickest way for a supervisor to lose his employees' respect.

Management Training

Management training, as we know it today, perpetuates the Litany of Management, and by doing so it is steering literally millions of management men in the wrong direction—a direction that is stifling their careers. I'll explain this shortly, but first let me say that some proportion of management training is useful. I very willingly acknowledge the value of training managers and supervisors in specific techniques that are pertinent to a person's responsibilities. Certainly the Production Control Supervisor, for example, should be well versed in data processing and inventory control. This type of directed training can help persons better understand their jobs.

The management trainers, however, have wilfully traversed the wavering line that separates the practical and beneficial from the wasteful and useless. Production men are subjected to courses in research management while scientists attempt to master cash flow techniques. Even worse, *all* management people are required to waste hours of their time absorbing communications theory, sensitivity training, and human relations theory. These courses are as useful as winking at a pretty girl in a dark room. The best way to learn to communicate, to learn to be sensitive and to learn how to handle people, is on the job. I know a manager, for example, who just returned from an intensive six-day course in sensitivity training. He confided in me that he had learned much about himself during that time. His greatest fault, he said, was the impatience he displayed with the foremen reporting to him. But now that he had acquired insight into his behavior and the reasons for it, he felt he was better equipped to handle this aspect of his relations with the men reporting to him. He appeared to have gained a great deal of self-confidence. Two days after he told me his story I happened to be walking through his department. Lo and behold, guess what I saw. This very same manager who had supposedly overcome a grievous fault was yelling so hard at his foremen that his face had suffused with blood and his eyes were bulging in their sockets. I thought he was going to keel over. Those six days had helped him indeed. (Incidentally, the management training courses don't come cheap. This course, I was told, cost the company $750.)

Management training assumes a more ominous tone when it misleads managers about their purpose in the organization and their approach to getting a job done. This whole book attempts to debunk the Litany of Management, and as we have come to see, the Litany is propagated by management training. For example, the leadership manuals blithely ignore guerilla tactics, infighting, and the like. They do not prepare managers for the onslaught of phonies and cutthroats. They preach the conventional verities such as are described in the Horatio Alger model. *They deliberately stay away from those subjects that are most important to the aspiring supervisor and manager.* The manager who allows himself to be misled by all this horseshit is woefully unprepared to tackle the hard realities of business life.

Being put on the job, being allowed to make decisions and mistakes, learning from the mistakes—all these allow managers to grow and develop into genuine contributors. Unless managers are forced to think for themselves, they will not learn. And all the training in the book will not help them, not one tiny bit.

Democratic Management?

Democratic management is at the very core of the Litany. And while almost everybody pays lip service to it, in reality democratic management does not truly exist.

If it did then why are all organizations headed by *one* person? Why do we appoint a *chairman* for a committee?* Why is *one* individual appointed to run a task force?

Let's establish this one point clearly: Every organization is run by one person who has the ultimate responsibility of making decisions. The rest of the group has the responsibility of helping its leader arrive at the proper decision. Take, for example, a task force which has been established to tackle the imposing job of cost reduction. Besides the chairman, there are representatives from manufacturing, purchasing, accounting, industrial engineering, and production planning and control. Each representative advises and contributes according to his own specialty. In the end the chairman weighs all the evidence presented by each member of the group, and then he makes a decision. Not the group—him.

Real democratic management assumes that each person's vote is equal, and that each person has a vote in arriving at decisions. But that can never be the case, and there are solid reasons why not.

The implicit reason is knowledge of the subject. Obviously, the accountant is knowledgeable about standard cost methods, the industrial engineer's expertise is work methods, and so on. The value of any individual's contribution will depend on his expertise in the matter. Next, the degrees of skill and conviction must be considered. Each member of the group has different skills and each has varying degrees of conviction about the matter

---

*This assumes, of course, that a leader has been appointed. Sometimes, in an effort to diffuse responsibility, that isn't done.

at hand. Finally, the matter of accountability is of paramount importance. Who is going to bear the responsibility for the recommendations advanced by the task force? In normal practice this is assigned to the chairman of the group.

All of these variables cannot be reflected by a distribution of votes, particularly because each situation is fluid and opinions change. It takes a leader to meld the recommendations of the group into a cohesive whole and establish a sense of balance in the decisions made. Therefore, the leader is the one to make the final decision, and in his hands rests the success or failure of the task force.

Because of the almost immutable acceptance of the Litany, managers must pretend to adhere to the practice of democratic management, silly as it is. To conduct working sessions of the group in an autocratic fashion is tantamount to inviting the wrath of the gods. Rather, the careful manager does what's really best —he listens carefully and weighs the opinions and contributions of each member of the group. If he didn't, he would be guilty of discarding some potentially beneficial ideas, and by closing his mind he could wreck the group's chances for success. If the leader is accomplished in the art of listening, not only can he generate more positive results but he will also be credited for being a democratic manager.

The Fallacies in Theory Y

Management social scientists have no sense of balance. They propound interminable theories of organization which, they feel, explain the entire spectrum of human nature and behavior. And once they have their latest goodie they are smugly prepared to accept it as the ultimate panacea in human relations. No further knowledge need be sought. The millenium in human relations has arrived.

Throughout the history of management social science one plateau after another has been scaled, and in each case the management theorists have genuinely believed that utopia has been reached. While it cannot be denied that each new theory of human behavior has helped advance our knowledge, certainly we are a long, long way from that ultimate day when the newest theory achieves a utopia of sorts. Frankly, I don't really believe that day will ever arrive. What is important, however, is that we strive toward that goal—intelligently.

In the meantime, every latest theory is hailed as the insuperable and unassailable truth by the management seers. Unfortunately, there are always unexplainable deviations that cause the theory to be held in suspicion. But the theorists invariably shut their eyes and fervently hope that the doubters will vanish.

The apparent danger for managers is that they will fully subscribe to the latest dictum and foolishly and blindly attempt to install its sacred teachings on the shop floor. Of course, the real disillusionment starts then. The ultimate hardnosed test of any theory of management rests in its effect on people in actual working conditions. If it works, fine—human understanding has been advanced a notch. If it doesn't work, it's just liable to create havoc among the guinea pigs, and the guy that gets it in the neck is the manager who didn't first carefully think out the ramifications of the theory before he allowed it to be installed in his department.

Look at it this way. Theories of management can work in individual companies while different theories will work equally well in other companies. Robert Townsend, for example, used methods that were eminently successful in running Avis. But when Avis was later merged with ITT the same methods were no longer appropriate. ITT itself uses vastly different methods than were used at Avis, but that is no criticism. ITT is one of the best run and most effective companies in the world today. One has only to look at its almost unbelievably sustained earnings record to recognize that.

Yet the management theorists blatantly refuse to accept what is apparently staring them in their collective faces. The "new" theory becomes an obsession, blinding them to the realities. All other approaches to human behavior automatically reach the stage of obsolescence almost overnight, while the new theory is welcomed as profusely as the second coming.

A cogent illustration involves the Theory X/Theory Y assumptions of human behavior. Douglas McGregor, in his book, "The Human Side of Enterprise" contrasts the traditional approach, which he calls Theory X, with the new approach to human behavior, which he calls Theory Y. Theory Y evolved as the new plaything of the social science set during the last decade. Enthusiastically they welcomed and accepted every facet of Theory Y while bemoaning the tragic consequences befalling those managers not astute enough to part with the traditional approaches. Within management circles, as centered about the Personnel Department, Theory Y has gained full recognition, displacing every iota of common sense about the handling of people.* Let's examine some of the more common assumptions of Theory Y and see if they hold water for *all* situations as the theorists would have us believe.

---

*I do not quarrel with many of the human behavior assumptions made by McGregor. Actually, many of them have added immeasurably to our understanding of people. But I do question the wholehearted endorsement of *all* of what McGregor has to offer simply because much of what he says makes sense.

1. *People don't have to be forced or threatened. If they commit themselves to mutual objectives, they'll drive themselves more effectively than you can drive them.*

Basically, this is true, and it becomes more unarguable at succeeding levels of the organization. The magic words here are "commit themselves." Unfortunately, people, and most particularly those at the bottom of the organization, have either lived out or totally abandoned their dreams or aspirations in terms of organizational commitment. When that occurs, the ability to commit themselves to company goals withers commensurately.

2. *External control is not the only means of bringing about effort toward organizational objectives. Man will exercise self-direction in the service of objectives to which he is committed.*

I think the whole point is missed here. It's not whether man will exercise self-direction. Of course he will. But that shouldn't mean that we allow him to run willy-nilly on his own sweet way. What happens, for example, if he is a general manager running a five million dollar segment of the business and he makes a six million dollar mistake? The entire business goes down the tubes, right along with the jobs and careers of its employees. Prudent business judgment tells us that it is sensible to follow up on the performance of subordinates for two basic reasons. First, as in the example just cited, a subordinate could make a costly and irrevocable mistake. Careful follow-up, without stepping on the man's toes or breathing down his back, is warranted. Second, consultation on important corporate matters will give the man the opportunity to broaden his base of knowledge and understanding about several business matters. This helps develop managers of high effectiveness.

3. *Once man has reached an adequate subsistence level, money ceases to be the prime motivating factor. Higher needs then become paramount.*

What would your reaction be in a situation where you were being interviewed for a job and the Personnel man told you that they don't pay much but they do respect the dignity of the individual and they believe in personal fulfillment?

I'm sorry. I won't print such language, but needless to say, your reaction is typical and predictable. Whenever the behaviorists or their counterparts in Personnel open their mouths and exude such slop as dignity, fulfillment, and the like, the fact remains that money talks—and in a voice so clamorous as to overwhelm all pipsqueak considerations. The first law of management states that to attract and keep good people you must pay well; to keep them motivated you must pay well; and when superior performance is noted you must pay well. Good men naturally gravitate to those jobs where the money is. If you attempt to motivate them with Theory Y, you'll probably wind up with mediocrities.

In summary, there is much good in job enrichment, human relations, Theory Y, etc. All new theories have their place in the business environment. But their fruitful application presupposes hard thought on the part of managers committed to company goals.

Scrooge and the Pay Raise

Some contemptible managers do not believe in awarding full salary increases to a man being promoted. Instead they give him half of the money due him when he is promoted and tell the man, "Jimmy, you do a good job and I promise you the rest of your increase in six months." These disappointing words are often accompanied by a hearty slap on the back and a loud exhortation to "get things done, Jimmy."

Jimmy can have only one reaction to this vile, penny-pinching attitude: Regardless of the promotion and regardless of admonitions to himself to do the best he can, he will not go all-out in his efforts. He can't. Put yourself in this man's shoes and see how *you* would feel. He is working for a corporate scrooge, and his best recourse is to use the new promotion as leverage to find a better-paying job and a new boss who understands the importance of rewarding a man justly.

Once Jimmy has the new job he can then walk calmly into his former boss's office and give the man proper thanks for his generosity, in words similar to these: "Here's my two-weeks notice, you penny-pinching bastard."

Paychecks Come First

Let's put things into perspective. A paycheck may not be the only reason for people working, *but it's the first and foremost*.

So for God's sake, if one of your people does not get his paycheck, or his paycheck is inadvertently shorted, *get it corrected the very same day*. Don't let Accounting tell you to wait for next week or even tomorrow. There isn't any valid reason that I have ever encountered for not making immediate corrections.

Do it!

Fringes for the Foremen Too

A particularly colorful tinge of green is exposed whenever someone from outside company management encounters management fringes. That envy is shared by the labor force, social do-gooders and also some members of the public at large, to name only a few.

Dining room privileges, reserved parking, company cars, first-class air travel, generous expense accounts, and the like are often criticized on the grounds that they generate a privileged management class. And to some extent they do.

But what in the world is wrong with that? Management fringes are a positive way for a company to reward its management, and they can make the job that much more enjoyable. People on the firing line deserve recognition, and not just in their paychecks.

My only gripe about management fringes is that they don't extend all the way down the management line. The poor foreman, scissored between the demands of his wage people and the policies and goals of his management, deserves as much consideration as the vice-president of his division. I'm not saying that every first-line supervisor is entitled to a company car. Not at all. These privileges, by necessity, must be graded according to contribution. But why can't he have a reserved parking space and a seat in the company dining room? Why must he travel tourist, while his boss makes the same flight sitting contentedly in first class?

We constantly criticize European companies with their rigid, inflexible caste system. We do the very same thing, only we don't say we're doing it.

Management fringes are a great motivator. But only if we include *all* members of management.

It's a Man's World

Some managers I know carry lipstick and powder with them to work in the morning. But don't allow the cosmetics to fool you. Female executives in American business today are tough, competent, and determined to overcome the shallow bias and hearty male snickers that accompany women's every move. I am referring to women in supervisory and managerial jobs, as opposed to secretaries, clerks, and technicians. These women—the professionals—are still something of a rarity in business, although the barriers are beginning to lower, and women are finding increasing acceptance within executive suites.

Professional women have been confined largely to the fashion and retailing industries, but more and more of them are appearing in scientific and technical jobs in a variety of other industries. Scientists, in general, have been more liberal in their recognition of women within their peer groups than men in other fields of endeavor.

There are reasons why women have been discriminated against in business. In addition to my exposure to the thinking of many businessmen on this subject, I have directly supervised professional women in industry for several years, so I can relate my first-hand experiences as well. Let's examine some of the objections to women competing with men on the professional level; a subject, incidentally, that is usually ignored by writers of the conventional Litany of Management.

Women are too emotional to think straight

This is nothing more or less than a sop for the male ego. There are no major differences between professional women and professional men. Some women are too emotional to think straight; so are some men. The *real* professionals, both men and women, are steady, cool, and objective. It is true that women, taken in general, are more subject to emotional responses than men. But women in business—the professionals—do not normally permit their emotions to interfere with their work. They manage to confine or, at least, mask their personal feelings while they are on the job. When you come right down to it, women can be just as tough as men when the job demands it.

Women use tears as a weapon

Not the real pros. If professional women use tears to get their way, they don't deserve to be managers. Most of the women I have supervised have never shed a tear on the job, even when they have been subjected to the most relentless pressure, and even when they have been told in no uncertain terms that their proposals or suggestions were not to be considered. And don't kid yourself. I have observed some men under similar pressures lose control of themselves, yelling and ranting. I don't believe that you can predict the response of individuals to pressure situations on the basis of sex.

Women prefer working for women

Baloney! There's nothing women hate more. They would much prefer to work for men. Men are much more sympathetic to women then women are. There is little pity in the heart of one woman for another, at least in a business situation. Women supervising women are tough, demanding, and ruthless, regardless of the thin veneer of smiles and cordialities they exhibit. While off the job they might be terrific friends, but when they clock in at 8:00 a.m., all mercy is swept down the drain. In many respects, having women supervise women is a vastly superior organizational arrangement to having men supervise women; particularly at the first level of supervision.

Women are not career-minded

Dispel that myth immediately. Don't confuse the young married secretaries with older professional women. The latter group is highly motivated. They have to be. Either they are single and supporting themselves or they are married and helping to support a family. In many instances, female professionals are the major breadwinners for the family. In any case, they are in business for a purpose—just as men are.

Women use sex to get ahead

This happens sometimes, but only because men permit it to happen. It's difficult for women to break into the management ranks, but if a woman is physically attractive she will find it easier to dissolve the barriers. Sex is a potent weapon in the female arsenal, and it is sometimes difficult to blame women for using it to their advantage. There are so many false and artificial barricades erected against the advancement of women in business that they instinctively realize they must use every weapon at their disposal. The male manager who allows himself to be influenced by sex is several cuts below an effective administrator and deserves to be fired—or even better, to lose his job to the woman that used him. After all, she outwitted him.

Women in business are enslaved and shackled by the same feeble prejudices that are used to control blacks. Inequities in the areas of pay and advancement are common. The manager who permits himself such bias is robbing himself of good people.

Blacks in Business

I don't know why the hell people get so uptight about blacks in business. I've seen *people* (black and white, male and female) who can do a job and *people* (black and white, male and female) who can't. Those *people* (black and white, male and female) who can't do a job I've tried to get rid of; those *people* (black and white, male and female) who are capable I've tried to push ahead.

I'm not attempting to disentangle the complex issue of racism here. It's just that a manager has the obligation to get results, and therefore must judge an employee on his or her contribution. Racial reaction, pro or con, throws that judgment off; the manager either feels that the black is entitled to keep his job irrespective of performance, or he demands too much and is too critical. Big-hearted managers and bigoted managers are equally culpable. To be effective, a manager must divorce himself from emotional, subjective judgments and concentrate on developing capable subordinates.

Unwritten personnel policy hasn't helped much. Lately, personnel departments have been under a lot of pressure to hire blacks. Typically, they have responded to this pressure by informing department heads in the company they service in this fashion: "Joe, you've only got seven percent blacks working for you. The national average is about ten percent, so you've got some catching-up to do. That means that the next three people I hire for you are going to be members of a minority group." So instead of being allowed to choose from the best of *all* possible candidates, Joe now has to play catch-up ball, choosing from a considerably narrowed selection. This is not fair either to Joe or to the person he hires—particularly if he is black.

But now that the doors are open, let's examine some of the common fallacies that corporate people have attributed to the black manager.

A black manager is a risk

Yes, that's true, particularly when you compare the advantages he's received with the advantages of his white counterpart. Take, for example, the black colleges in the United States today. Mostly, they have meager resources and token support from industry. Naturally, most of their graduates will not be on a par with graduates of most other academic institutions. Companies sincerely wanting to hire blacks are going to need patience, and they will be the kind that want to invest in the development of people.

A black manager will not be accepted

Don't you believe it. If he is the type of person who can fit in with your group, right away he has a strong advantage. Chances are that you will be evaluating this characteristic when you interview him. But let's assume that he has a somewhat abrasive manner. Won't that tend to keep your staff from accepting him? Of course it will. And then the only way he can gain their respect is by his determination to do a good job and his ability to perform. If he is a winner, then regardless of his color your staff will work with and support him.

Blacks make better specialists than supervisors

It is a fact that many companies tend to make blacks into specialists, rather than supervisors. They sometimes even create staff openings for them. In too many instances blacks aren't permitted to become supervisors because of the unspoken fear that white people will not do good jobs for a black supervisor.

This is utter nonsense. I have first-hand experience to disprove that. In a large and conservative company I once worked for, blacks supervised production and clerical people and black managers supervised first-line foremen. Most of them did a good job; some of them didn't. In all respects their performance was similar to what you would expect from the entire spectrum of white supervisors.

A black will demand better treatment than anyone else

If he does, bring him firmly back to earth by telling him that what he gets will depend on the job he does. He will earn recognition; it will not be granted because of his color. If he refuses to accept this, find yourself another man.

Part Five

GETTING THERE: SELECTING THE RIGHT JOB

> *Some of our best executives have been abject failures who were fired out of Company A for being no damned good before they went to Company B where they have been outstanding.*
>
> A Director of Psychological Testing for a large American college.

Admittedly, it is difficult for a man on the outside to recognize the inner character of a corporate enterprise, and to estimate how he will feel about it after six months or a year. But the effort is worth making. The man who is able to form a cool and detached opinion of the industry, the company, and the line of work that is offered can go far to protect himself from selecting the wrong job.

What, then, are the crucial tests of suitability? Each manager must set his own standards, but the fundamentals of the problem are the same in all cases. The articles presented on the following pages are devoted to this subject. They provide a means by which a manager can bring strategic insights to bear on any job that he is considering. By broadening his appraisal of a job beyond the salary offered and the promises made, such tests can go far to reveal dangers that might otherwise slow down or damage his business career.

Mating of Man and Company

A man entering a new company can have an impressive reputation as a performer, be thoroughly knowledgeable about the company's product line, and yet soon find himself beset by the possibility of failure. He may unknowingly stumble into a position that he cannot handle because he has made a fundamental error in strategy; an error that has produced the all-too-frequent mismating of man and company.

How, then, does the manager select that position that adequately matches his talents and personality with those of his potential employer? If you follow the recommendations offered by the Litany of Management you are liable to become confused. The conventional wisdom cites so many conflicting rules that a person can easily get bewildered and make a very costly career mistake.

My experience and the experience of several knowledgeable businessmen can be distilled into the guidelines presented in the following sections.

Company Environment

Virtually all experts in placement work will mention the importance of determining the company environment before anything else. Is it aggressive or static? Is it somewhere in between? Industries toward the static end of the scale include banks, insurance companies, utilities, and, of course, governmental agencies. At the opposite end of the scale are the fast-paced, quick-changing industries such as automotive manufacturing, retailers, and cosmetic companies. Those industries require a great many fast decisions regarding production, styling, marketing, and pricing. Managers in those businesses live by their wits, guts, and imagination. They *always* know exactly where they stand. If they don't respond fast and effectively, they're out of a job.

Trouble starts when a slow, thoughtful banker-type becomes embroiled in a financial job with a cosmetics concern. His responses aren't anywhere near fast enough and he soon makes a mess of his job. The toughened, aggressive automotive production manager, on the other hand, would die a slow death working for most government agencies. He couldn't stand the turtle's pace. Managers in steel companies tend to be strong and decisive, like their products. In the financial community, far from the smokestacks, the requirements are for smoother, more polished types.

Economic Climate

A manager accepting a job with a company that has financial problems had better be fully aware of that fact. If he's a slow starter, he's in trouble. Tempers are always shorter in such a company, and newcomers are allowed damn little time to prove themselves.

Company Age

During the various stages of company growth, different types of managers are needed. A young company needs enthusiastic, hard-driving men who feel comfortable wearing two hats and who don't particularly give a damn about plush offices and fancy trappings. Ten years later, the same company will have completely different needs. The same men who were so effective in the early period may find their toes lopped off for being out of line, or they may become bored for lack of challenge.

Manager's Orientation

The manager heavily committed to manufacturing may find his upward path blocked in a company where general management positions are awarded to men in sales or finance. In a similar vein, the mechanically oriented manager may be out of place in a bank. The point is clear.

The Boss and the Boss' Boss

There are two cardinal rules that obviate all the baloney written about superior/subordinate relationships in a new job situation. The first is concerned with the "chemistry" between your potential boss and yourself. Does he like you? Do you like him? Can you trust him? Do you think alike? Do you feel at ease with each other? Do you communicate well with each other? I realize that chemistry is a nebulous characteristic. It's something intuitive, something you feel. *But it's the most important consideration.* You can be the greatest manager going, but if this chemistry isn't there, then you're gambling on a relationship between your boss and yourself that could be in trouble before it even starts.

A manager can recognize the importance of the right chemistry with his boss, but sometimes he neglects to think of his relations with the boss' boss. It helps if the chemistry is there too, but it doesn't have the same significance. What's important here is similarity of backgrounds. In other words, does he talk your language? Is he sympathetic to your ideas? Does he have knowledge of your field of work? If so, then you can communicate with him; you're both on the same wavelength. When you later propose changes to your boss, he, in turn, won't have any difficulty selling it to his boss. That could be of vital importance to you.

Titles Are Important

Many of the businessmen I have known scoff at the importance of job titles. They have been heard to say: "Job titles. Pfui. Give me the money any day. A big title and thirty cents will get you a ride on the bus."

Don't you believe it.

Titles are very important to a businessman, but he doesn't know it because he has once again been fooled by the Litany of Management. I am not referring to the prestige value of titles, nor am I concerned with the fact that the director's office has a better carpet than the manager's office. These are superficial considerations. A title really matters, however, when a businessman is looking for a job and needs all the leverage he can muster to make his next position the best possible. Certainly he stands a better chance of becoming a vice-president if his present job title is director rather than manager. The meanings of both titles are significantly different to most businessmen.

A personal friend of mine—call him Bill—once worked as Manager of Administration for a medium sized concern. He reported directly to a Vice-President and his organization was a large one, handling all accounting, financial, purchasing, and contract work for the company. In most companies he would have been called Director of Administration.

My friend Bill had a stroke of bad luck. As often happens today, his company merged with another company, and Bill, through no fault of his own, found himself out of a job. When he started looking for a new position, he found himself more hampered than he would have thought possible simply because he was not labeled as a director. Two companies he talked with needed a vice-president of administration, but they would not consider Bill because his current job title did not indicate that he had had any responsibilities at the director's level. When Bill attempted to explain that, in effect, he had been a director without the title, they listened politely but did not offer him a job. As Bill mentioned to me later, if he had at least been called a Corporate Manager of Administration, then he might have been in the running. The title of manager turned off both companies because they visualized its holder as having a very definite place in an organization—at least in their organizations—and that place was two notches below vice-president.

Ultimately Bill was forced to settle for a job which carried the title of Director of Administration, doing exactly the same job he had been doing when he had been called Manager of Administration. He said that his career plans had been set back about two or three years because of the earlier misleading title.

Don't let that happen to you.

Do You Like Your Company's Products?

"What kind of work do you do, Daddy?"

"Well, son, I'm an engineer."

"What do you engineer, Daddy?"

"All kinds of machines that make things."

"What kind of things?"

"Well, son, er, we make birth-control pills."

"What are birth-control pills, Daddy?"

"Well, son, those are tiny pills that, ah, well they, that is—"

Sweat it out, Dad; you'll never make it.

If you're ever in the position of poor Dad, finding that it's hard for you to talk naturally and enthusiastically about your company's products, then you may be another hapless victim of the Litany of Management. There isn't a damn thing wrong with making birth-control pills unless you happen to be ashamed of the product.

The conventional wisdom urges the businessman to fully disregard any liking or preference for company products when he selects a company to work for. To support that argument the Litany claims that a professional administrator can ply his trade in any industry, that his skills are wholly transferable, and that any product preference severely limits the choice at hand.

Discard that tripe as you would discard most of what the theorists proclaim. It is a self-deceptive attitude, sounding practical on the surface, but without a morsel of truth to it. The concept of the professional administrator is, in itself, highly doubtful,* but there can be little doubt that a person works more energetically and with more satisfaction when he truly likes the product or service to which he contributes. Mechanically oriented managers are inclined to give that little bit extra to their jobs if their companies are producing machine tools rather than drugs. The man who is excited by the publication of books is not likely to be properly motivated if his work is in the electronics field.

I was once offered a production job with a well-known maker of women's girdles and bras. Concurrently, an automotive company had asked if I would be interested in working in their automotive assembly plants. When I weighed the comparative advantages of each offer, it looked as if the girdle and bra company could give me a little more of what I wanted in the way of career objectives. And yet, I hesitated. Something held me back from accepting the job with the girdle and bra firm. I was puzzled because I didn't quite understand why I was holding back. And

---

*See the section on "Job Knowledge vs. Administrative Skills."

then it dawned on me. It finally came down to the fact that I was not overly enchanted with the prospects of manufacturing ladies' undergarments. It just didn't do anything for me.

I felt rather foolish about my attitude, but nevertheless I discussed it with the plant manager of the undergarment company. I told him that it had been a very close and hard decision and that I had decided to accept the offer of the car company. I explained that both jobs could offer me a lot, but I thought that I could utilize my hobby of car mechanics to advantage. He got a little hot and told me that I was being foolish and it was simply immature to allow personal preference for products to interfere with my job objectives. When I left his office he was sneering at me. Needless to say, after his talk, I began to doubt my conclusions.

I no longer harbor those same doubts. Now, more than ever, I am convinced that any manager owes it to himself to try and work with a company whose products hold his interest. If he's in a business that doesn't stir his imagination, he's most definitely at a psychological disadvantage. Unless he's able to find zest and pleasure in his work, the job can become dry and unsatisfying. Over the years this can make itself felt in his contribution to company efforts, and ultimately in the rewards he receives. It is only realistic for a man to pursue what interests him. The incentive to do a job is greater and so are his chances for success.

Do You Look Like an Executive?
or
The Importance of Image

It's time for a little clinical experiment. Imagine, if you will, two naked managers standing before you. One man stands 6'2" at 195 pounds and the other is 5'6" tall weighing 155 pounds. Now dress the smaller man in a $39.95 plaid suit, a flashy $1.79 tie purchased from a discount house, and a $10 pair of moccasins. Adorn the taller manager with a Hickey-Freeman suit, a white-on-white dress shirt with double cuffs, an imported but conservative silk tie, and $40.00 Nunn-Bush shoes. Now stand back a few paces and ask yourself this: "If I knew the job capabilities of both these men to be about equal, which one would I select to work on my staff?" Unless you look like the smaller man or dress like him (you're disqualified; you've got an axe to grind), chances are that you would most certainly select the taller and better dressed man. Be honest.

To most management people image is very important, and how a man dresses, what his bearing is, how much he weighs—all these can have a very significant effect on his job success. Size, dress, and stature are valued commodities, and a manager sometimes feels better when he knows that his supervisors are tall, robust replicas of Grecian gods. There is an all-pervasive feeling that taller men in $200 suits somehow command more respect than their more diminutive counterparts on the job. Although that conclusion is both arbitrary and unfair, it is amazing just how prevalent it is.

I know a top-level manager in a large company who is prominent in his field. He has successfully directed the new product efforts of his firm for many years. When he speaks of selecting a candidate for work in his division, that candidate must possess something more than the expected technical skills and competence. In the manager's own words, "In my line of work, how

a man looks is sometimes just as important as the job he does. I would rate both characteristics on the same level of importance. We interface with almost every division in the company, and on many occasions my people are required to make presentations to the board of directors of the company. If I send a man to make one of these presentations who doesn't have the necessary bearing or stature, I'm liable to adversely affect my chances for approval of the project I'm trying to get started."

Over the years this manager has developed what he considers a nearly infallible way to aid personnel departments in selecting the right type of individuals for his department. As he put it, "I have developed a height/weight ratio scale. By referring to any range of heights I can tell just how much a man should weigh within a few pounds. This assures me that I don't wind up with some obese person who would be particularly repugnant to other important people in the company. Of course, regardless of the weight, I don't permit any man to be much less than five feet six inches tall. Executives just don't respect men they have to look down to."

Shades of bias!

In many cases, like the one cited above, the absurdity of the use of image is obvious. But don't fool yourself. More management people subscribe to these fallacies than you may realize. While publicly they proclaim their willingness to hire and promote anyone with ability, privately they believe in the importance of image. I have worked in a company, for example, in which all the first-line supervisors looked like a long row of Hollywood pretty boys. Those guys were all about 6'1" and 190 pounds, had curly hair and sparkling white teeth, and dressed to kill. Any visitor on a tour of that plant would have thought he had accidentally ventured onto a movie set.

Is there a current preference in managerial physique? The answer is yes. The fashion nowadays is for tall, lean men, preferably with a little gray in the hair around the temples, and the start of crowsfeet at the corners of the eyes (denoting maturity and experience). Other physical aspects of the aspiring manager must also pass muster. These are:

Face Is it puffy or fat? Are there any pimples showing?

Eyes Does he flutter his eyes when he talks? Is there any sign of a nervous tic? Are the eyes bloodshot? Does he look you right in the eye or does he avoid your direct glance?

Bearing Does he stand straight and true? When he sits down does he flop into his chair?

Nails Is he one of those nervous individuals who bites his nails? Does he keep them clean and well manicured?

Hair Is his hair too long? Does it touch his collar? Is there a cowlick? Is his hair neatly combed?

If you happen to be 5'6" and are about to have a stroke while you're slouched over in your chair reading this and biting your nails, please don't let it discourage you. Many smaller men have made it to the top and more will continue to do so. Granted you will have to combat a bias that is infinitely more subtle than that directed against blacks and women in business. But you can do it. One word of warning, however; take a look at your peers during your first day on the new job. If they all look like Robert Goulet, then get out the old resume and polish it up.

Transfer Happy

I worked at one time for a major automative company where the order of the day was frequent transfer of managers. The division I worked in had 20 plants spread across the country. Whenever a new plant manager was assigned to a plant, and that was quite often, the shuffle would begin. Inevitably, one of his first jobs was to bring in "his people." The current managers of production, engineering, production control, quality control, and accounting would soon find themselves scrambling for the same or similar jobs at other locations in the company. As you would imagine, personal contacts were very important. They normally meant the difference between a good and bad location and a good or bad job. Very few of the current managers on the plant manager's staff would be able to retain their jobs without moving to another company location.

Now the managers from the other automotive plants would begin arriving. For the most part, they were men who had previously worked for the plant manager at different plants, and they were favored by the plant manager for many varying reasons. Usually, but not always, the managers would move to the new plant in a higher level job.

To my knowledge, and I knew all the plant managers in the division, none of these men would last at any given plant for much longer than two or three years. That was about the average, although I personally knew of three plant managers who stayed five or six years at one plant.

Let's add up some of these numbers. Each plant staff was composed of approximately 20 key men, including the plant manager. With 20 plants in the system, and assuming that plant staffs changed every two years or so, 400 top men in the division would be transferred in that time. That's one hell of a lot of transfers. In my own experience, I was transferred three times within a four year period, each time on a promotion, and each

time at the specific request of a plant manager. One plant manager I followed from Detroit to California to New Jersey. And one location—in Ohio—I worked at for only three months.

It seems to me that all of this movement of people around the country is entirely unwarranted; at least when the transfers occur every two years. A company cannot adequately rationalize the transfer of management men simply because a new plant manager has arrived on the scene. Not only is it pure hell for these men and their families, but it also means waste and inefficiency for the company.

Neither can I believe that most transfers are related to job failure. It is not reasonable to assume that every two years 20 plant managers have failed to do their jobs, nor is it reasonable to assume that an additional 400 managers have been stumbling through their responsibilities. That just doesn't make sense.

I cannot help but believe that the mass of transfers in that company, and many others like it in other companies, is based on a "let's shake them up" philosophy. This school of thought equates job insecurity with job performance, the latter being dependent on the former in proportionate amounts.

I call it "transfer happy." Frankly, it's not a very pleasant existence, particularly for the married man with children. If you should ever find yourself in a similar situation, and you are not the type that enjoys packing up and moving around the country every few years, then get out while it's still to your advantage.

The best time to discover management's attitude toward company transfers is during the job interview. It's rather easy to do. First determine how many locations the company has. If there are several plants or offices, try to find out just how often transfers are expected. The best way to do that is not by asking the question directly. Unfortunately, there are personnel men who'll lie like hell to get you on board if they feel you're right for the company. Don't be naive and risk your career on that chance. Instead, during the process of being interviewed by the three or four people who will talk with you, inquire politely about the number of company locations. Then say something like "Oh, I know Atlanta well. The plant there is located at the west end of town, isn't it?" If your man has been there, he will then tell you about the plant. If he hasn't, he might start talking about some of the other plants. If that approach fails, try asking him for a comparison of the plant you are in with the other plants in the system. His answers will be revealing. When he starts to describe the other locations, ask him if he has worked there. You'll soon draw him out and get the information you need to know. It won't be particularly difficult to discover how many of the company locations he has worked in during his years with the company. Then you can easily determine how many years he has with the company. He'll be happy to tell you that. People love to tell you about themselves. That's your tipoff. Divide his number of years with the company by the number of plants he has worked in. If it comes out to less than five years per plant, watch out. You might find yourself working for a company that is transfer happy.

Part Six
STAYING THERE: TECHNIQUES FOR SUCCESS

Handle your tools without mittens.

Benjamin Franklin
Poor Richard

Much of what you have read so far has contributed to your understanding of business realities. Several techniques and suggestions have been presented for your consideration, but there are many more. In fact, there are so many that it is hard to think of them all. But they all have one thing in common: the shedding of the deadweight of illusion and the ability to maintain a sense of proportion on the job.

If you can think back to when you were a young person, and if you can remember climbing a tree, then you know that the hardest part was getting up the trunk. The first several seconds counted the most. You would try to shinny up the tree, maybe even skinning your knees in the process, until you reached the first strong branch. Then it was comparatively easy. That's the way it is in business. In the early years as a young manager, before you've got a secure foothold, you need all your strength and agility just to hang on to what you've got. Part six is devoted to explaining those concepts and techniques that will show you how to straddle that first strong branch before your competition does.

Put Them All in Production

Every manager should have the opportunity to work in production for at least one year. It doesn't make any difference whether the person manages an engineering activity or a clerical operation. The one year or so in production will teach him many business truths and he will be a broader, more responsible person and an improved profit contributor as a result.

The production function molds top performers. A production man learns quickly that time is one of management's most precious assets, and so he learns to be stingy with it; to pack every available minute with beneficial activity. A production man becomes adept at mustering all of his available resources—men, machines, materials—into the best combination for meeting his cost, quality, and delivery goals. A production man soon develops the ability to focus on what is significant. He establishes priorities. A production man learns how to respond to and handle people problems with more deftness than his counterparts in staff work. He has to; his goals are more stringent and more time-demanding. He cannot afford the luxury of moving along at a slower, more leisurely pace.

A production man, then, learns to get the job done. Can anyone argue the necessity of instilling this most vital ingredient in *all* managers? How many times have you observed an experienced mechanical engineer design an unworkable, esoteric fixture? In how many instances have you watched one of the so-called experts from data processing provide less than meaningful reports to production? How many times has the employment manager sent lackluster, undesirable candidates to be interviewed for production jobs?

A staff manager with production time under his belt has enhanced his chances for success on the job. He is also in a more favorable position to help guide and train his staff in developing job effectiveness.

This same line of reasoning can, and should, be applied to the marketing arm of the company. In marketing the salesman is the equivalent of the production man in manufacturing. Both have direct line responsibilities. All other marketing management men (product management, advertising, distribution, promotion, etc.) should have the opportunity to work for a period of time in the field as salesmen. That experience will enable the marketing manager to do a better job in his own specialty. It will help improve his contribution to company efforts, and in the process he will become a broadened individual.

Dealing with Unions: The Only Way

So you're dealing with the union, and you've read every text and listened to every talk you possibly can about how to deal successfully with them. Invariably you have been told to be honest and forthright in your approach. Invariably this tactic has failed. You scratch your head, genuinely puzzled. It appears as if the Litany of Management has failed you again.

Step back, if you will, and think for yourself. Forget all the junk that you've been taught over the years. Discard the training manuals and wipe your mind clean of the slop that has been pumped into it by well-meaning but foolish instructors. Start with the job steward, the union representative you deal with. Ask yourself if he is honest and straightforward with you. Ask yourself if his motives are purely unselfish or if they contain a trace of self-aggrandizement. You know instinctively what the answer must be. The steward is an elected official; and because his fate rests solidly in the hands of the union membership, he will—he *must*—do what he can to get his way in any dealings with you. He has to look good to his membership—while you have to look good to management. And if you obey the Litany by attempting to be completely honest and play the game by his rules, he's going to wind up looking a lot better than you do.

Your only recourse is to find out what the man really wants, not what he's telling you but what his real aim is. This may not be as easy as you think. For example, he may approach you all upset, demanding that a machine operator be transferred to a similar machine in another foreman's section. He may argue that the operator does not get along with his fellow workman on the adjacent machine. The steward is subtly appealing to your desire to maintain harmonious relations within your department. You think this is a really solid idea, and without any further thought on the matter, you acquiesce to his demands. He leaves, apparently satisfied, and you think you have heard the last of the matter.

Unfortunately, you've been had. You have acted like a virgin sacrifice in an ancient Aztec temple.

The steward returns the following day with a similar complaint, but with two different machine operators. The same request is made again. About this time your suspicions are aroused, but only slightly. After a prolonged discussion during which you raise a little hell with the steward, you let the operators change places again. If you don't grant his request, you will be accused of showing partiality toward some operators, and that you can't afford. When he leaves your office you get an uneasy feeling in the pit of your stomach. Something is coming, but you don't know what it is. To your relief, the steward doesn't bother you for the next few days and the incidents slip gradually to the back of your mind.

One week later the steward approaches you with a job rotation schedule. This schedule graphically depicts all the machine operators in all sections of your department rotating from machine to machine on a daily basis. The steward claims this to be the most equitable arrangement. He fortifies his argument by saying that some machines are harder to handle than others, and that it is only fair to rotate assignments by machine operators within a given occupational class.

This is too much for you to take. You blow your cool while the steward calmly smokes a cigarette and watches you behave like an idiot. He has made you look bad and you both know it.

After you regain your composure you remind him that there has been no historical precedent to permit rotating on machines. You hastily scan through the labor contract although you know there is nothing in that document covering job rotation. You present him with this information. All this time he is sitting with his feet propped up on your desk, smiling at you, not saying anything. You get scared. This is not like the steward you know.

Then he drops the bombshell.

Because you stupidly permitted the rotation of machine operators on two different occasions, the steward claims that you established a precedent. You argue that you had reasons for allowing the men to rotate and that, in itself, does not constitute approval of job rotation. But inside you feel sick. You know you've been tricked, and you know you've lost this one, and you know you're going to look damned silly in the eyes of your management. And you're right.

Now look at your management. Ask yourself if they believe everything the union representative claims. Ask yourself if their prime consideration is always to support your decisions and the decisions of your foremen, the men on the firing line. The answer is all too apparent. Management *must* look out for itself in precisely the same manner that stewards take care of their own. That's the way the system is. You're fully aware there is a great deal of horsetrading involved when top management and union leaders meet to settle grievances and bargain on contracts. Well, it's no different on your level.

As a department manager or as a first-line supervisor you are caught between two parties with opposing views. As a member of management you support and enforce company policies and regulations. But you are the hapless party that is subjected to all the strife and sweat generated by union/management conflict. Your role is a tough one—in fact, one of the toughest, so it stands to reason that any move on your part must be well thought out. You cannot act precipitously. Neither can you respond to union demands as if they sprang from a deep well of understanding and mutual trust. To do so is sheer suicide. On the other hand, you cannot afford to reject union demands arbitrarily, without giving them the consideration they deserve.

What you can do—what you *must* do if you are to survive and progress—is to keep cool at all times; approach your relations with the union with an open mind, but don't be naive, start thinking for yourself.

Details are Important

Part of the Litany of Management declares that managers must take an overview of their operations and leave details to their staff members. That strikes me as pure, unadulterated folderol. In my experience, managers who neglect details are soon looking for other jobs. Contrary to the accepted folklore, meticulous attention to detail, so-called minor matters, usually indicates sensitivity to quality of products and services, good organization of jobs, careful delegation of responsibilities, and thorough follow-up.

That does not imply that managers who observe these standards are required to follow every detail themselves. It means that they are conscious of the importance of detail and provide for the handling of it. It means that their organizations understand the importance of detail and appreciate its significance. In business the amateur fondly reminisces about his achievements —while the professional carefully evaluates his mistakes. Many golfers, for example, live all week with the pleasant memories of the few good holes they played on the previous weekend. The pro golfer, however, mulls over the one or two bad holes he played. He continually examines the minute details of his game.

Lack of attention to details is a sign of sloppy work habits which breed sloppy thinking. Poor housekeeping in a plant or office invariably indicates wasteful and costly operations. The personal carelessness of a manager is quickly emulated by his staff. Failure to establish and maintain standards throughout the organization can easily result in erratic and mediocre output.

Job Knowledge vs. Administrative Skills

There is a dogma in the Litany of Management that says a good manager can move from industry to industry and do a competent job without requisite knowledge of each business; that job knowledge (knowledge about products and processes) is secondary to organizational savvy and administrative skills.

Don't allow this foolishness to blind you to the realities.

It is true that a competent manager without job knowledge has a better chance for success than the manager who possesses job knowledge but has little administrative skill. That cannot be argued. But the Litany of Management commits a sin of omission here—it fails to point out that the greatest manager going will quickly lose his effectiveness unless he thoroughly learns about his company's products and processes.

The manager in the *best* position is the one that has both administrative ability and job knowledge. That is a potent combination.

Job knowledge is power. Without it, the conversion of management's resources into tangible sales and profits is mediocre, at best. Few executives in their right minds would think of attempting to run a business without a staff of people competent to handle all the technical aspects of the company's operations. Managers without the prerequisite technical knowledge will not survive. The manufacture of airplanes and the operation of commercial airlines, for example, are no jobs for amateurs. The development, manufacture, and distribution of pharmaceuticals cannot be entrusted to unqualified hands. The entire computer field demands specialized abilites. And so it is with most other businesses. Technical competence, coupled with administrative skills are accepted without question as basic requirements. Each manager must have a full technical understanding of his products and processes to be effective in making the right administrative decisions. Without adequate job knowledge, administrative skills falter and perish.

Some Thoughts on Mistakes

It goes without saying that people who make mistakes are people who are trying to make things happen. The adroit manager will learn as much from his mistakes as he learns from his successful decisions. Be careful of those people who do not appear to make mistakes. Either they are passing the buck to the other guy or they are not doing their jobs properly. Neither type will contribute much to the organization.

Let's look at mistakes from another perspective. As many successful managers know from their own experience, progress comes with certain built-in risks. A good case in point is the first scaling of Mt. Everest, some years ago. A mammoth feat, it never could have been accomplished except for the unsuccessful efforts that preceded it. Mt. Everest could not have been scaled any sooner because certain mistakes had to be made and certain things had to be learned before man could know enough to conquer it.

There's one good thing to remember about mistakes in American industry: volume absorbs many errors. Companies, despite a multitude of mistakes, keep plugging away, stolidly and fearlessly gaining more and more ground, making more and more profits, satisfying more and more customers, shareholders, and employees. The smart companies waste no time worrying about bridges that may never be crossed, or errors that some people would call failures if they were permitted to brood upon them. This positive type of thinking leads to undisputed greatness.

Decision-Making at Home
or
Ma Bell and Me

There was a time when I prided myself on the frequent business calls I received at home from my staff at work, even those calls arriving at two a.m. Now that I look back, it's obvious that I welcomed the calls because they were ego-satisfying. In effect, they proclaimed the dependence of subordinates on my decisions rather than their own. That, of course, was caviar for the soul.

I no longer welcome calls at home. My people are required to make their own decisions. It didn't take long for me to realize that my bloated self-esteem was limiting the personal growth of people on the job, interrupting my family life, and blindfolding me to the realities of how I was being used.

It's only natural that if the boss actively wants to make all the decisions, then his people will gladly let him do so. Not only is he the boss whose wishes are to be respected, but it lets his people off the hook. They sigh with relief. Let somebody else handle the hot ones!

The only way supervisors grow into managers, however, is to make their own decisions. Decision-making demands tough and disciplined thinking; without it people get soft and flabby and scared of responsibility. This is not to say the boss shouldn't be accessible to make those decisions only he can make. Not at all. But all others should be made by his people and nobody else. That's how people grow and learn to do the right things.

Keep your hands off that phone!

Every Manager a Salesman

One thing is abundantly clear about the manager's role in today's business environment: He must deal with scores of people to get anything done. Obviously, if he doesn't learn to talk in terms of other people's interests, he is not going to be particularly successful in promoting his ideas.

The Litany would ask you to believe just the opposite. It solemnly declares that a manager must subordinate his interests to that of the team, and in general submerge his personality within the team.

That's just fine—provided that the ideas of the manager and the team coincide. However, they seldom do. Each team is usually composed of individuals from different operating and staff groups within the company. The accountant is interested in cost, the production manager in maintaining schedules, the quality control supervisor in quality, etc.

A manager is *always* selling. Everything he does is open to review by all kinds of people with vested interests. If he's interested in promoting his views and proposals it's imperative that he gain allies and supporters. He has to keep peace with people at all levels of the organization at all times. Needless to say, that is tough to do.

As he climbs the organizational ladder he encounters more and more often the frustrations of having to sell his viewpoints. But he becomes increasingly adept at the practice. Let it be noted that he would not rise in the organization if he failed to perfect the arts of selling. While he seemingly pays tribute to committee management, his dedication is an equable facade. He listens as if he really liked to and suggests rather than orders—and he half persuades himself that he is just suggesting. But he is just playing the game.

How does he go about selling his ideas?

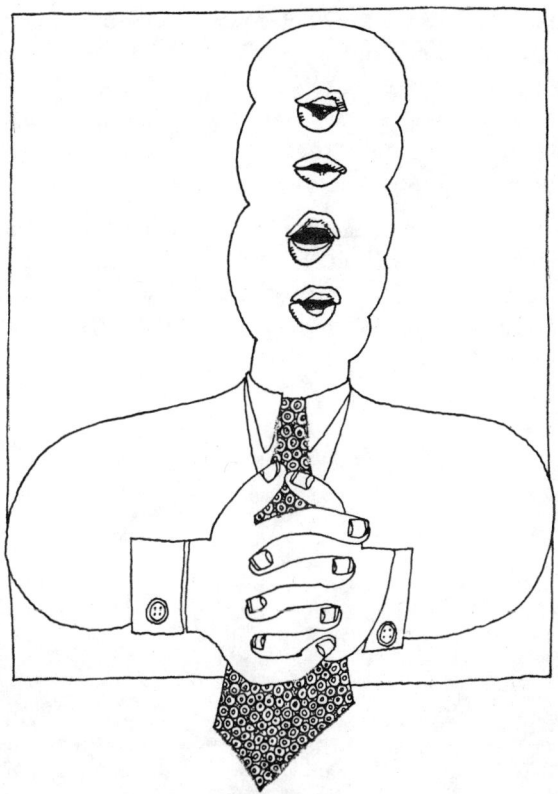

If he is the type that can sway groups of people, then he presents his ideas before a committee. Using a well prepared talk, he charms and persuades until everyone (at least, those who count) will enthusiastically support his plan.

Some managers, however, are ineffective when dealing with more than one person at a time. These managers must concentrate their efforts on individual presentations. This method is also appropriate in situations involving several people, some of whom may actively oppose the manager. By discussing the matter with one person at a time the manager has the opportunity to persuade each individual before that individual's opinion has been reinforced by other people's suggestions. In using this approach the manager is relying on a behavioral law: People are more receptive to an idea if they are unaware of any opposition to it. The manager has the chance to block off the reinforcing actions of opposing individuals.

Every manager must decide for himself which approach is more productive for him; selling the group or selling the individual. But sell he must, however he does it. Today's corporate environment stresses the attribute of persuasion (selling), and the manager needs to become professional at it.

Address Yourself to Plumbers
or
Words and Phrases That Hamper Communication

There is a tendency for people in management to speak in deliberate understatement, using pretentious words and phrases. It probably makes them feel important. But all types of jargon, inside talk, and just plain gobbledygook impede the flow of honest communication. To illustrate what I mean, let's stroll through some typical corporate halls and listen to some of the talk. I'll translate as we go.

What they're saying	What they really mean
"Gentlemen, I believe the time has come for us to amalgamate our resources."	"For Christ's sake, let's stop fighting and get together."
"If we restructure the existing organization there is an excellent possibility of recouping our losses."	"Whoever set up this screwball organization should have his head examined. Now we've got to start from scratch and keep our fingers crossed."
"I think this problem can best be approached by establishing a committee with representation of all concerned parties."	"I don't know what to do, either. Let's get out of this fast."
"The time has come, gentlemen, to define the parameters of the existing situation."	"Will somebody please tell me what's happening?"
"Certainly we are at the stage where we can finalize this problem."	"Can't any of you guys get the job done?"

What they're saying	What they really mean
"While I can't argue with your rational approach to this situation, I am somewhat wary of it. Call it a subjective judgment."	"Regardless of what your goddam computers say, I've got a gut feeling the whole bottom's going to drop out."
"The time has come to maximize our talents and resources."	"I'm going to try like hell to get the most out of you lazy bastards."
"Our management skills inventory did not reveal anybody from your group ready for expanded responsibilities."	"Those lazy slobs in your department couldn't run a hot dog stand."
"I most seriously doubt the efficacy of that approach."	"Listen, sonny, the goddam thing won't work."

A good deal of management jargon may result from pomposity or from a wistful desire to sound learned. Much of it results from inability to think clearly and directly. Certainly, most of it is attributable to the amicable facade that management demands from its employees; a sort of unwritten law dealing with "getting along with people." Whatever the reason, it can only create roadblocks in the communications path.

The inevitable result of distorted communications can be seen in the story of a city plumber who had cleaned out some drains with hydrochloric acid and wrote a commercial laboratory asking if there was any possibility of harm to the pipes. He promptly received the following reply: "The efficacy of hydrochloric acid is indisputably established but the corrosive residue is incompatible with metallic permanence." The plumber was proud to have received an answer and thanked the laboratory for approval of his method. The dismayed laboratory rushed another letter to him, saying, "We cannot assume responsibility for the production of a toxic and noxious residue with hydrochloric acid. We beg leave to suggest to you the employment of an alternative procedure." The plumber was more delighted than ever and wrote to thank them again. By this time the laboratory got worried about what might be happening to the city's sewers and called in a third man, an older scientist, who wrote simply, "Don't use hydrochloric acid. It eats hell out of pipes."

The most promising way to avoid slipping into management jargon is to pretend you're addressing plumbers, directing them in simple language how to do a job. You'll soon find yourself talking plain language, easily understood by plumbers and corporation presidents alike.

Treat Them Equally

One of the most difficult problems young supervisors and new managers have is that of being consistent in their relationships with people. This common fault is due mostly to the manager's relative inexperience in business, and is normally corrected with time. That it *must* be corrected cannot be argued. Those who continue to display inconsistencies in handling people seldom advance in an organization. They cannot be trusted with expanded responsibilities. Some learn this fact early in their careers, while others are slower to grasp its necessity and meaning. It is the latter group who suffer the most. What may be abundantly clear to you and me doesn't penetrate their minds at all. A young supervisor who once worked for me, Bob, had this peculiar disorder and it continually manifested itself in his dealings with subordinates. For example, Bob would grant time off to one technician, while a different technician making the same request for a similar reason would be denied. When I asked him why the double standard, he grumbled that the technician denied time off was a poor worker.

Poor Bob had a lot to learn. He didn't understand the effect of his inconsistent actions. While he was simply attempting to reward good performance and punish bad performance, he was actually creating a negative atmosphere in his department. The technician whose request was denied got hopping mad while the technician whose request was granted noticed the inconsistency and thought the boss was playing favorites. Result: two employees soured on the boss.

Consistency is related to appearance as well as action. While it is vital to be consistent in handling people, it is also important to maintain a consistent facade. Granted it is only human to have our ups and downs, managers have the additional burden of keeping these peaks and valleys well hidden. A boss who is euphoric one day and disgruntled the next day, and shows it, will confuse those people working for him. They may be hesitant to approach him on a bad day, and even worse, since they never know when his mood will turn, they may *never* approach him with their problems. The results of these actions are all too obvious.

Don't confuse the *treatment* of subordinates with the *handling* of them. This is often where the theorists become thoroughly mixed-up. All employees should be treated equally but their handling will vary from person to person. While it is expected, for example, that plant rules are to be uniformly enforced, the application of disciplinary measures which deal with infractions must be handled according to the circumstances of individual cases. If both Jimmy and Bob have violated the same plant rule, it may be the best approach with Jimmy is a good chewing-out, while Bob's behavior can be redirected through a gentler counseling session. It all depends on the individuals involved.

Keep Your Sense of Humor

A close friend of mine once related this experience:
"A company I worked for early in my career had an unwritten rule which forbade laughing and too much smiling. Most people obeyed the taboo and walked around wearing particularly severe and glum expressions. When I first started working there I thought the atmosphere comparable to a morgue. The top management people had such deadly serious expressions that I wondered what their faces would look like if they found out I had made a mistake. It wasn't pleasant to contemplate.

"One day, after I'd been there a few weeks and the strangeness had begun to wear off, I walked into the foreman's lounge to get a cup of coffee, and as you would expect, my expression showed dead earnestness, just like everybody else's around me.

"There were only four supervisors in the lounge, all sitting together, drinking coffee and talking. As I walked toward the coffee machine, I tripped over an extended table leg and went sprawling belly-down on the floor of the lounge. It hurt like hell and I guess I looked up with a pained expression that sent all four guys into an uproar. They laughed so hard that tears came to their eyes. Watching them was infectious and I soon was joining them until we were all on the floor, laughing uproariously and practically gasping for breath.

"After we'd all regained our composure, I found myself relaxed and in good spirits for the first time in weeks. The common bond of laughter established a camaraderie among us that I had not found since joining the company. All of us shared a warmth that was decidedly foreign to the chilly atmosphere we had been working in. It wasn't too long after that I decided I was in the wrong company. I found within myself a sense of humor that I did not want to smother. Within six months I had found another job with a company that was more tolerant of human warmth."

It is unnatural for people to keep joy and humor suppressed. When management people are unable to laugh and smile, tensions build, and coming to work in the morning becomes a very unpleasant task. People who are conditioned to maintain a facade of grim determination eventually sour, and their real spirit approximates their outward expression. A dry rot sets in.

Since that gruesome experience my friend has made it a habit to smile and to express his sense of humor, and even to laugh at himself when it's warranted. He says it can make a world of difference in your outlook, and I believe it.

Hero Yesterday, Bum Tomorrow

The object lesson of the heading is: Don't rest on your laurels. Companies reward managers for the good job they are doing today, not for what they did last year. Top management has a short memory, and justifiably so. Companies can survive only by meeting the challenges of the present and the future. Yesterday's achievements are like yesterday's follies: better dead and forgotten.

Avoid Emotional Reactions

I will be the first to admit that it is supremely difficult to completely divorce emotion from business affairs. We spend approximately one-third of our day at work, and it is not the easiest thing to turn off emotions for eight hours and then let them take their natural course for the rest of the day.

However, it must be attempted, and the manager must be, at the very least, moderately successful at it. Emotion is the antithesis of thought, and thought is the prime tool of the corporate manager. Acting under emotion does not make for sound and wise business decisions. The aspiring manager must always remember that his adversaries will attempt to provoke an emotional response from him, and we know that that can be extremely dangerous. The manager must train himself to act *only* after his moves have been motivated by cold, rational thought. Any other response can be sheer suicide.

Sometimes a manager is justified in displaying emotion—but only after he or she has decided rationally that an emotional response is the tactic indicated. For example, the manager may be attempting to bargain with a union representative. After carefully feeling out the man he may decide that the only way to get his point across is to put the fear of God into him. Then, and only then, is the manager justified by acting in an emotional manner. But remember, it's only an act.

On the other hand it is important for the manager to avoid acting like a cold fish. He may have to think like one, but to act like one with his associates is another matter altogether. Nobody wants to work with a human computer. People simply do not feel comfortable in the presence of a scheming mind. The manager who is too businesslike will not engender warm feelings in others. People just naturally feel more comfortable working with a personable manager. It makes them feel more secure.

The astute manager also focuses on issues and facts rather than on personalities. He never allows an issue to degenerate to name-calling or personal attacks. Rather, he directs his thinking, and the thinking of those around him, toward the issues at hand. He recognizes that personal attacks only arouse emotional antagonisms, and these antagonisms die slowly. They can only rupture communications and relationships among people who need to work together.

Books on Management Development

Many of the books published on this subject aren't worth the paper they're printed on. Any manager wasting his time and money on them deserves what he gets. Too frequently they offer ten or twenty golden rules that are supposed to transform human-relations ogres into human-relations marvels. Any attempts to put these gems to use are often wasted; sometimes even catastrophic. Let's face it. People can generally smell a phony a mile away, and any manager who suddenly turns 180 degrees in his handling of people becomes very suspect in their minds. The *only* way to get along with people is to have a genuine respect for them and an understanding of their motivation.

The manager who starts with that can enhance his own ability to handle people through experience coupled with some *good* management reading. I would recommend these books on the subject of getting things done through organizations:

1. *The Human Side of Enterprise*, Douglas McGregor, New York, McGraw-Hill, 1960.
2. *The Effective Executive*, Peter F. Drucker, New York, Harper & Row, 1966.
3. *Managing For Results*, Peter F. Drucker, New York, Harper & Row, 1964.

And for those dewey-eyed novices who want to know what working with people is all about, I would recommend:

1) *Survival in the Executive Suite*, Chester Burger, New York, MacMillan, 1964.
2) *Executives Under Fire*, Chester Burger, New York, MacMillan, 1966.
3) *Business as a Game*, Albert Z. Carr, New York, The New American Library, 1968.

These six books are not the only good books on management that are available, but they are certainly the best ones I've read on the subject. They sum up years of meaningful knowledge in the area of working with people and getting things done. They should be particularly helpful to the young man new in the business world as well as to the experienced manager seeking advancement.

Part Seven
MOVING AHEAD: DOING THE RIGHT THINGS

If a man reaches the top, he is not going to tell you how he got there.

A vice-president of a large
American corporation

In the modern corporation the personal influence exerted by a businessman counts for a great deal. A manager who knows how to increase his influence within his company is well on the way to rapid advancement. Where an outstanding success in corporate life is found, the person is usually a master of respect-winning strategy.

Of major importance to any hopeful business career is the manager's ability to make his personal quality felt by those people he works with, and to use this quality productively in getting a job done. Not only must the aspiring manager learn how to motivate people, he must also know how to hire, promote, and even fire when necessary. There are certain proved techniques to get the most from people; the best of these are described on the following pages.

Hiring People

So much has been written and said about hiring people, and so much of it is contradictory, that it is very easy for a manager to quickly become confused, do the wrong thing, and hire the wrong person.

I have found no foolproof way of assuring 100 percent successful selection. Regardless of how much screening and interviewing, checking and double-checking is done, mistakes will be made. No one has yet found a way to predict with unfailing accuracy how people will perform in a particular situation. (Incidentally, if your personnel man tries to convince you that his method of selection is infallible, mark him down as a phony and avoid him like the plague.) How a candidate is going to behave on the job can only be estimated, and the job itself may differ from advance descriptions. Personnel can make tentative predictions, but there is still a strong element of chance involved.

Like famed Ponce de Leon in pursuit of the forever-elusive elixir of youth, I chased for years after the one perfect method of selecting people. I read avidly the available books on the subject, and at one time or another I attempted to put their theories to use. Regardless of the method used I still was not batting one thousand; in fact I was far from it.

In the final analysis, each manager has to find the most suitable method for himself. I have raised my batting average considerably by seeking to learn three things during the job interview: Does the applicant's experience qualify him for the job? Will his personality fit in with those of other members of the organization? Is he motivated to succeed? Anything beyond these three points is strictly a fringe value. It may have interest and supplementary value, but its importance is secondary. By concentrating on the candidate's answers to the three questions I have learned much that I need to know about him.

There are a few techniques that can be used to evaluate the candidate during the interview. In the opening minutes, observe closely whether he is aware of his surroundings. He should be fully aware of you and the environment around him. A person not aware of his surroundings should alert you to a possibly complacent personality. The man who is wrapped up in himself can't function effectively because he isn't fully aware of where he is and what he's doing.

In the same vein, notice whether the candidate asks questions or docilely accepts everything you say without comment. Find out if he has a history of innovations to improve the performance of his job. The questioning, inquisitive man is the one who will think out goals, problems, and solutions.

Whatever you do, however, don't attempt to trick the man. Remember, an employment interview is a trying experience, and most people are nervous when they are being questioned, however politely. You can find out all you want by honest questioning and investigation. Also, when the man is describing his background, you will have the opportunity to closely evaluate his responses. For example, does he get his ideas across? When he talks about his previous jobs, does he accentuate his accomplishments or does he talk about his duties?

How much does he want the job? How strongly is he motivated to succeed? How important is achievement according to his personal standard of values? All of these questions can be asked directly, but his words will reveal considerably less than his manner, his attitude, and his past employment record.

Finally, for better or worse, a decision must be made, a candidate accepted, a previously vacant job occupied. Only time will tell whether the decision was a good one. You have only one other thing to aid you.

You cross your fingers and hope.

Selecting the Best People for Promotion

Selecting the right individual to be promoted from within your organization is nowhere near as difficult as selecting someone from outside the company. The new man is a mystery. What he has achieved in previous jobs is not a matter of first-hand knowledge. You can only abide by first impressions, what he tells you, and the response you get during telephone calls to his former employers.

The man within your organization is another matter entirely. You know what he can do; you've observed him under fire. Nevertheless, there's always that nagging doubt, that reluctance to commit yourself without proof positive. You say to yourself: "Well, he has done a good job. But can he handle the opening one rung higher in the organization?"

You will never have that 100 percent assurance. Mistakes will invariably be made. But the man in your company who has done a good job and who is ready to tackle a bigger job is always the best bet. If he has the well-deserved reputation as a winner, then his staff will rally around him.

Nobody wants to work for a loser. People are afraid that management will associate them with the failures of an unsuccessful leader. The solid reputation of your man will encourage his staff. If he has done a good job before, his chances for success in the new job have been greatly enhanced.

Firing People

Firing people is one of the most despised tasks of the organization and, at times, one of its most necessary duties. The sheer unpleasantness of this job is compounded by the realization that the manager who must do the firing is the very same manager who hired the man to begin with.

As I mentioned before, in "Hiring People," a manager's judgment in selecting people is fallible. First impressions of people are often wrong. The man who looks like a tiger and who starts out the same way can fizzle out after a year or two. Even though there are ways of testing individuals to see how they act under fire, none of them is equal to putting a man in a position of responsibility where he has to make good or else.

Keeping a failure on the job is unfair to other people who could do the job, as well as to the company. Mostly it's unfair to the man himself; the man who cannot do the job. Any person holding down a job that he is unable to do is tense, angry, and frustrated. This situation is almost certain to affect his health and his family life.

To hire or promote somebody for a job does not entail any obligation to keep him on that job if he does not succeed. For the individual appointed, the opportunity carries with it a very specific obligation to make good. If he does not, there is no sound reason why he should feel he has a guarantee to be kept on the job.

Without doubt some people will think that attitude excessively harsh. Yet the survival of a private firm in the business world depends entirely on the performance of its management team. Private companies that are successful are rewarded by continuing in business. Private companies that are unsuccessful go out of business. Therefore, the company that tolerates failure invites catastrophe. It cannot survive.

When someone is not performing on the job there are some common-sense guidelines to help the manager reach a decision:

1. Admit the mistake as soon as possible.
2. Verify the judgment made through consultation with others.
3. Discuss the situation frankly with the person concerned.
4. Warn him, put him on probation, and provide help for improvement during the probationary period.
5. If insufficient improvement is shown, fire him.

When a manager fires someone he has the obligation to tell the man why. If that isn't done, the person could make the same tragic mistake again with another company. Letting the man know he is through can be done without needlessly injuring his self-respect. Tell him that a person with different skills is needed for the job and, as diplomatically as possible, tell him what those skills are. Give him adequate time to find another job and then let him announce to the organization that he is leaving to pursue another opportunity. This will let him save face with his associates.

Appraisal Techniques that Build Managers

If you harken to the all-knowing utterances of the Litany of Management, then you will accept the drivel that the task of the manager is to mold his people into dynamic performers. This implies that the task of the manager is to change people.

Far from it. The real task of the manager is to multiply performance of his people by making whatever strengths and aspirations they have work for the organization. The effective manager is very much aware that one cannot build a strong organization on weakness, or by attempting to correct the weaknesses of strong men. To achieve results, one has to muster all available strengths—the strengths of one's associates, subordinates, and self.

The problem of correctly appraising the strengths of the organization is highlighted during that time of year when performance reviews are being made. Unfortunately, most performance review procedures are directed toward correcting weaknesses rather than building and utilizing strengths. In one form or another, they conclude by stressing action taken to assess and correct the employee's "outstanding needs."

This backdoor approach is detrimental to both the employee and the company. It is completely unrewarding. I know a manufacturing manager who prides himself on rating his people. One time when we were discussing rating techniques he whipped out a form from his desk and proclaimed proudly: "I personally developed this appraisal sheet. It contains those 20 characteristics I consider are needed in the makeup of a good supervisor." He went on to tell me that he carefully rated each man for all of the characteristics listed on the form, and that any deficiencies he noted about the supervisor were closely followed-up between rating periods.

Of course, he had completely missed the point. A manager should never ask "What can a man *not* do?" but rather "What can this man *do well?*" During rating periods he should look for excellence in one major area, and not for the "rounded man."

President Lincoln was once told that General Grant, his recently installed Commander of the Army, was a lush. His reply was: "If I knew his brand, I'd send a barrel or so to some other generals." Before he had chosen Grant, Lincoln had appointed several Generals whose main qualifications were their lack of major weaknesses. They had been recommended for their ability to do many things adequately, and stay out of trouble. As a result, the North had not made a dent in the Southern armor for the three bloody years from 1861 to 1864. In sharp contrast, Lee had staffed wisely from strength. Every one of Lee's generals, from Stonewall Jackson on, was a man of monumental weaknesses. Each of them was, however, endowed with one area of real strength, and it was this strength alone that Lee utilized. As a result, the "well-rounded" men Lincoln had appointed, were beaten time and again by Lee's men, the generals of narrow but very great strength.

Any attempt to staff and build an organization to avoid weakness will end up at best with mediocrity. The idea of the "well-rounded" man with all strengths and no weaknesses is pure Madison Avenue propaganda. People fall in love with their words and management writers are no exception. Phrases such as "whole man," "mature personality," and "well-adjusted personality," are words only, and when they are applied to people they become fiction. Too often, people who fit those descriptions are mediocre—even incompetent—performers in business.

To use the tool of appraisals effectively, then, managers concentrate on strength. They ask themselves: "What can this man do?" "How can he best contribute?" Only when his weaknesses detract *substantially* from his strengths do they concentrate on eliminating weaknesses. But most of all, they understand that to build strength they must tolerate some weakness.

The Final Step in Behavioral Correction

There comes a time in every manager's career when he encounters one particular subordinate who fails repeatedly to respond to direction or authority. The subordinate, for one reason or another, doesn't appear to give a damn and it looks as if he is headed for early "retirement" from his company. The manager has attempted to turn this man around and he has just about exhausted his entire repertoire of motivational techniques. At this stage failure is staring him in the face.

I would like to mention one final approach which has been neglected deliberately by the Litany of Management. Try this if you will:

Lay aside the textbooks on behavioral psychology, forget for the moment the maxims of McGregor's Theory Y, brush aside the permissive attitude surrounding employee relations, get the man alone, and *chew his ass until you've shaken him to the goddamn core*. This sorely neglected method of correcting performance can work miracles if you will but give it a chance. In behavioral situations it is the equivalent of shock treatment for mental patients: a last resort.

Needless to say, you're not going to find this technique described in your favorite management training manual; and it wouldn't surprise me to find it's turned the Personnel Psychologist's hair white when he hears about it. But here it is, presented most probably for the first time in print. And, if you're honest about it, you know it has worked miracles in situations you have witnessed or experienced yourself. Use it with discretion, make it part of your bag of tricks, and you're going to be surprised just how effective it can be.

Management by Objectives

After 50 years of fumbling efforts the management theorists have evolved what promises to be their most fruitful discovery—that people like to work. Before this notable revelation, organizations had been built on the premise that every job and every task should be reduced to the level of childish simplicity to allow any idiot to do the work at hand. To compensate people for that gross insult, they are still offered rewards such as vacations, pension plans, medical benefits, insurance, and company-sponsored recreation. *This combination of elementary work and bountiful rewards has oriented people to enjoyment away from the job.* Silly, isn't it?

The management theorists are now reversing their concepts. They have come to realize that: (1) people can contribute to company efforts willingly, (2) they want to feel the satisfaction that comes with doing a good job, and (3) results can best be achieved by creating an atmosphere in which people will commit themselves to the job without being forced or threatened. The new theory is called "Management By Objectives."

Management by objectives focuses on creating an environment that will encourage a deep commitment from managers to the company's objectives. It is essentially an approach to produce greater individual responsibility and improve the environment in which managers work. Each manager sits down with his boss and defines his responsibilities. They agree on objectives and the timing for their completion. Once that is done it is formalized in writing to serve as a guide for the manager and the organization. The manager is made aware that satisfactory fulfillment of the objectives is his baby. There is no attempt to assign objectives to a team. That would diffuse responsibility.

Now comes the hard part.

The manager's boss must commit himself to keeping his fingers out of the pie. Instead of breathing down the manager's neck to see how things are going, he should be obliged to let the manager fare for himself. Needless to say, this is not an easy thing to do, especially for the boss who prefers to follow-up and check every step of the way. The boss must realign his own work methods, and accept the premise that his manager will exercise self-direction in achieving the objectives to which he is committed.

Skeptics will ask how this concept works in actual practice. They may even repeat a favorite notion of the authoritarians: "People do what you inspect, not what you expect." Certainly this will be the case in a company that uses the conventional wisdom of force-feeding work to people. It needn't be; management by objectives can work quite well, but management must first create an atmosphere of trust and acceptance.

Before I am accused of going over the deep end to defend the use of management by objectives, let me say I believe it has its limitations. I accept the fundamentals of the theory wholeheartedly, but I also recognize that its application in American business must be planned and implemented carefully; otherwise the results could be disastrous. To tell the workers and foremen on a mass-production assembly line, for example, to plan their activities themselves would be sheer imbecility. Production would undoubtedly shrink to a mere trickle. On the other hand, to allow department managers full use of management by objectives may be very desirable. The management levels allowed to apply the theory must be so selected that the company will obtain full benefits.

Management by objectives allows people to grow and strengthens their ability to make the proper decisions. Not only does the job get done, but it's a great feeling for the boss to watch his managers develop into maximum contributors. It's marvelous to observe the transformation of a manager who depends on his boss for decisions into a manager who steps up to his own responsibilities. There are few satisfactions on the job comparable to that.

Try it sometime. It's fun.

Effectiveness vs. Efficiency: A World of Difference

What you do is far more important than how you do it.

Very little has been written about this sentence, but it almost invariably determines a manager's success or failure on the job.

Look at it this way: A manager must be effective. Most tests of managerial success indicate that this takes a number of different qualities, but they all boil down to intelligence, imagination, guts, and knowledge.

Yet, really effective men are conspicuously absent in managerial jobs. True, high intelligence is common enough, imagination is certainly not a rare commodity, men with fortitude are everywhere, and the level of knowledge seems to be high. But somehow these characteristics by themselves do not create the effective manager. Rather, they are natural resources that must knowingly be combined to produce results.

How then can a manager be effective? If you heed the solemn messages of the multitude of management training courses and books for management, the answer is simple. Learn to do an efficient job. Effectiveness and efficiency, however, do not equate. Efficiency defines the ability to do things right rather than the ability to get the right things done. The foreman on the line can always be judged in terms of quantity and quality of discrete output. His manager, though, cannot be judged by the same criteria. He is measured not so much by how he does things as by what he does. For example, at any given time a manager may have several problems facing his department, all contributing to excess cost. If he solves a dozen of these that are causing only ten percent of the higher cost, he has accomplished virtually nothing. If he works on two of the problems that are causing ninety percent of high costs, then he is doing something worthwhile. Even if he does only a fair job of licking those two problems he will have contributed more than if he had done an excellent job on the twelve smaller problems. This is the difference between effectiveness and efficiency.

Henry Ford is remembered for his development of mass production techniques for automobiles. At a critical juncture in the development of his company, he decided to depart from the common practice of custom building cars for the wealthy, and to produce a car that would both appeal to the majority of potential buyers and be priced within their budget. Mr. Ford could have marshalled his resources to produce a better hand-built, custom-made automobile. It is possible that he could have brought prices down somewhat in that way, but still not within reach of the millions of potential buyers. However his decision to mass-produce cars by the assembly line technique made accessible to the mass of consumers an item once out of their reach. The rest is history.

Being effective, then, means focusing on those items that make a manager's department competitive and viable.

Leave a Path Open

There probably are few things as dangerous as a cornered animal. Its reactions are unpredictable and it will act strictly in desperation. A cornered man exhibits the very same characteristics. He is both unpredictable and dangerous, and the man who has cornered him may find himself in serious trouble.

A manager should never corner anyone, not even an adversary. He should always leave open a path whereby both men can get together on their differences. This applies to words as well as actions. Verbal encounters can result in severed relationships just as easily as physical assault—and can sometimes be more dangerous than physical action, simply because the assault is on the man's ego. Because of this, always avoid ultimatums. They may appear to be irrevocable, and because of that, a person may not react to them in the direction intended by the manager.

If you tell a subordinate, "Increase your sales by ten percent or you're going to get canned," the first action of the salesman will be to look for another job. And, of course, while he's doing this, sales in his region will most certainly drop off.

If you're sending the same salesman off to a convention and you tell him, "Under no circumstances are your expenses to exceed $100," he is liable to assume that your position is totally inflexible. Suppose that, while at the convention, he has the opportunity to take out an attractive potential account for an evening on the town, but your words dealing with maximum expenses are burned on his mind and he drops the matter. Result: He may have passed up a chance to bring you back an excellent customer.

The right words can leave a path open. Suppose that in the first example you had said "Sales are off by ten percent in your territory. Let's find out why. Please take a few days to analyze the reasons, and then let's get together and discuss it." The chances are that you might have discovered the reasons for the sales decrease. In the second example it would have been better to say "Your expense limitation for the convention is $100. If anything unusual should occur where more money is needed, call me at your convenience. Otherwise, you are being asked to stay within the $100." Surely the salesman would have telephoned you, and recognizing the sales potential of the account, you would have authorized additional expenditures.

Use of words such as "maybe, perhaps, possibly, might" should normally be used in preference to "never, absolutely not, under no circumstances." If you leave a path open, you have paved the way for alternative actions that will help you achieve your goals.

Demand Excellence

The Litany of Management solemnizes the theory that people can be placed into three classes: the few who make things happen, the many who watch things happen, and the overwhelming majority who have no idea what has happened. The Litany goes on to say that all three have their rightful place in the organizational hierarchy, and that the dominant position will always be awarded to the first type of individual.

As I hear and read this tripe I can't help but feel intuitively that not only is it untrue, it is totally misleading. The manager who knowingly accepts second- and third-rate people in his department is rapidly speeding to his downfall. He can only be that type of person who accepts second- and third-rate performance. Such a person readily accepts excuses for not doing a job, and by doing so he dignifies failure.

To be successful a manager must demand excellence from his people as well as from himself. Frequently a manager complains that he can't do his job as it should be done because he does not have the necessary authority or because there is too much red tape and restriction upon his activities. This very same manager condones the alibi for nonperformance advanced by his staff.

The manager who makes things happen does not deal in reasons why something cannot be done. If he can't do it one way, he will try another. His one driving motivation is to make something happen regardless of seemingly great obstacles.

This very same manager gets off his ass and gets out there where things are happening. In the laboratory, on the production floor, or out in the field, this man is there, asking his people what can be done to do a job. He gets his people believing they can do what must be done regardless of the difficulties.

Making things happen becomes a habit with people who realize that excuses will not be tolerated. Demanding excellence, then, should become the *only* norm. People who achieve are people who recognize no barriers. They are ten feet tall.

Send Out a Scout

One of the prime maxims of military tactics can be observed when a combat commander sends out a scouting party before committing the main body of his troops to battle. This very same tactic can be used to advantage by any manager or supervisor in business and industry. Before he introduces a plan or before he advances an idea, he would be well advised to "scout" the receptivity of concerned parties to his proposal. Sending out a scout is a sound tactic and one completely overlooked by the Litany of Management, which advises in so many words, "Full steam ahead when advocating a course of action. Testing of the water is unwarranted. If the course of action is bad it will sink itself."

Undoubtedly that is true. A bad idea will sink itself. But so will a good idea if the timing isn't right or if management is unreceptive. The point is this: The manager could be considered headstrong or foolish if he attempts to have a proposal approved without first testing the water. In the eyes of management, he will appear to be a man who doesn't pay much attention to significant details. The attentive manager, on the other hand, will discuss the advantages and pitfalls of his proposal with representatives of concerned parties to assure himself that he has left nothing undone. That manager understands the importance of details. If some organizational opposition should be encountered as he quietly tests his idea, he will then be in a better position to counter the opposition when the proper time arises. By scouting the territory before committing his troops, he is in a position to adjust the plan, to help make it more acceptable to the organization. He can then commit himself through an official proposal, knowing beforehand that the proposal will be accepted.

Tight Budgets are Best

Are you plagued by thoughts of how to bring out the best creative mode of your people? The answer is simple: Plan a tight budget. A tight budget makes people rise to the challenge of doing the best job possible with their available resources. Give people unlimited or too generous funds and they will come up with less than top-grade results. With a tight budget they'll yell like hell and claim you're tying their hands, but once they're forced to respond to the challenge they'll surprise themselves by doing an excellent job. Tight budgets discourage empire building. (However, they must not be so tight as to create undue difficulties in getting a job done. See next article, "Time.")

Time

Some time must be set aside to plan for the future. Whether or not it is possible for you to do this during working hours is entirely dependent on your personal circumstances. *But it must be done!* It is not enough to devote your time to putting out fires. Responding to and working with the day-to-day exigencies is fine for the present. Somebody, however, must give thought to the shape of the organization as well as its duties for next year and beyond. *This is the job of the manager and one of his most common deficiencies.* The procedures, organization, and methods that are so successful today may be completely inadequate just a year or two down the road. The manager who fails to provide for tomorrow soon discovers that his department is unequipped for the battles looming over the horizon. Today quickly becomes tomorrow. It's something for all of us to remember.

Along the same line of thought, some managers base their plans on margins that are too tight for comfort. If everything goes well, the plans will be accomplished. But if something unexpected develops the plans could be partially or wholly missed. I know of one instance in which a production manager decided to meet a substantial increase in orders through overtime in his department. His plans to meet scheduled commitments were based on almost ideal operating conditions. No time was available to handle such contingencies as unanticipated machine breakdowns, excess absenteeism, and material shortages. It wasn't too long before he was forced to add a third shift—at the expense of missed customer promises while he manned and trained a crew for the workload addition.

Plans should always have liberal safety margins included. It is better to be ready for the unexpected simply because the unexpected almost always happens. The manager who tries to be a hero through habitual use of excessively tight planning normally gets in trouble.

Short-Interval Scheduling: A Tool for All Managers

As mentioned earlier in "Effectiveness vs. Efficiency: A World of Difference" it is very important for the new manager to distinguish between doing the job right and doing the right job. One of the prime benefits of Short-Interval Scheduling, or SIS as it is called in the trade, is its ability to focus attention almost automatically on doing the right jobs. It is a tool for all managers and supervisors who manage people.

What is SIS? SIS is a labor control technique that has been applied successfully in every industry and every type of job imaginable. For example, it has been used in banks and steel mills, airlines and photography studios, to name just a few. Specifically, it is a method of assigning a planned quantity of work to be completed by a specific time, and determining that the quantity of work has been completed within the specified time limit. The basic thought behind the system is simply: time is one of management's most precious assets. If a company can control 60 minutes in every hour for most of its employees, it can improve efficiency and profitability. SIS imbues each supervisor with the critical importance of effectively utilizing all of his available resources. It highlights substandard operations, thereby placing the supervisor in a critical area at a critical time—where he must be in order to improve operating methods.

Here is a simple explanation of SIS:

1. All work entering the work center is scheduled by one individual, who distributes the work for processing.
2. A reasonable amount of work is assigned to an employee who is told that this assignment should be completed within a specified time limit.
3. To eliminate delays in assignment of work, all workloads are scheduled in advance.
4. Performance is checked regularly (hourly, in most cases) to assure completion of work assignments on schedule, and off-schedule situations receive immediate attention.

Probably the most enticing advantage of SIS is that it instills in both workers and supervisors an immediate sense of urgency to get the job done. The effect is psychological and occurs because SIS establishes obtainable goals on a short-range basis. The frequent appraisals of performance ensure that employees will produce at, or close to, standard levels throughout the day. When daily output totals are the only guide to performance, a supervisor does not learn that an employee has not been turning in full performance until the day is over, and then it is too late to take corrective action.

SIS has its own, very unique methodology. It also has many more advantages than could be listed here briefly. I can only suggest that managers interested in the technique read my book on the subject: Short-Interval Scheduling, New York, McGraw-Hill, 1968.

Now That You're On Your Way----

When you're on the lower rungs of the company's organizational ladder, you may give little thought to the high-pressure competition necessary at the middle and top rungs. That is understandable. Even the comparatively ambitious tend to cherish the notion that life at the top is comfortable, and that decisions are fabricated in an atmosphere of cooperation and mutual respect.

That, at least, is the way it reads in the Litany.

More realistically, as you, the potential executive, start moving ahead of your rivals, you begin to learn that life at the top bears small resemblance to life at the bottom. At this stage you realize that you have committed yourself to a long and perhaps bitter battle. You can no longer afford that most delicious luxury of standing still and enjoying life. Those people who stand still do not survive at executive levels. You know that the climb from here on is going to involve you in increasing tensions.

It is hard to say when you will experience these feelings. Some men never know just when the moment of self-realization comes. But there will come a time—for most men somewhere between the ages of 30 and 40—when you will feel that you have made the irrevocable self-commitment. At this exact point you will experience a loneliness you never thought possible. If you've had the toughness of mind and spirit to make it this far, then you will know that the future holds clashes between you and your environment, and you will know that you must face these clashes alone. Your time for home life and outside interests will become shorter and shorter. In the middle of the crowd at the office you will be isolated—no longer intimate with those you have passed but not yet accepted by the elders you have joined.

At work the job of steering the right course will require more and more skill. And you will start to worry about status symbols. The overt differences in status and office amenities will be much less than you knew before, but the smaller the differences the more crucial they will become to you. You will find that it's easy to laugh at whether or not you have carpeting or tiled floors, or whether you have a silver or stainless steel carafe, but the joking is a bit strained, and a number of ulcers have been triggered by what would seem to be piddling matters to the disinterested observer.

"You achieve a certain position," one executive explains, "and you start getting scared that somebody else might take your job. You don't know who he is—it could be damn near anybody one step below you—so you take on protective coloring by faking to be the nice guy, everybody's pal. It's scary as hell".

The best defense against being surpassed, you will discover, is to surpass somebody else. But since every aspiring executive knows this, and since he knows that the others know it too, he can never really feel secure. You, too, will experience the same unnerving feelings.

Nevertheless, the rewards are commensurate with the pain. Prestige, luxurious working conditions, financial security, executive fringes—all of these make the trip worthwhile.

Well, you've made your decision. Keep your eyes open, think smart, and the best of luck to you.

Part Eight

NOW TEST YOURSELF AGAIN

Now let's see what you've learned. In the following series of multiple-choice problems, mark what you consider the best answer

Answer here

1. You are in a meeting which is considering the introduction of a product that you *alone* know the company is incapable of producing. As Manufacturing Manager for the company, you are fully aware that if the new product is accepted, your costs will skyrocket and you will be left holding the bag. You also know the company is hungry for new products. What approach should you take?

    a) Say nothing, look wise, and let the meeting run its natural course.

    b) Disclaim the new product and indicate it would be too expensive to produce.

    c) Suggest that acceptance of the new product be put in the hands of top management.

    d) Suggest that the product would enhance its chances for success by turning it over to Research for an extensive pilot-plant run and have the Accounting boys estimate costs of the product.

2. You are the Production Engineering Manager for your company. An engineer you hired a year ago has proved himself incapable of working with people. To complicate matters, this man is a top-notch engineer and he can handle the engineering aspects of the most difficult nature. Unfortunately he can't work well enough with people, and they have forcibly rejected all of his proposals. He has failed to respond to counseling. Your budget is not large enough to permit having the new man work by himself, developing ideas to be turned over to another engineer for implementation. What should you do?

a) Fire the new engineer.
   b) Transfer him to another segment of the business.
   c) Send him to a human relations course.
   d) Do the best you can with the man, recognizing the circumstances.
3. You have just discovered that the secretary you are having an affair with has also been having an affair with the company executive vice-president. In a fit of emotion she has declared her undying love for you, and vows to drop the other man. What do you do now?
   a) Continue enjoying the affair.
   b) Tell the secretary that while you think she is the most wonderful woman in the world, you are married and you must stop seeing her because your first obligation is to your six children.
   c) Keep your fingers crossed and pray.
   d) Shoot yourself.
   e) None of the above.
4. You are a Production Manager and you have just been notified by one of your foremen that a "hot job" is being run on a new piece of equipment that has no safety guards. The work cannot be processed anywhere else, and if it doesn't get out on time the company could easily lose a big customer. You evaluate the safety risks and find them minimal. What should you do?
   a) Continue processing the work as if nothing was wrong.
   b) Continue processing the work but tell the foreman to watch the job and caution the operator so that he won't be hurt.
   c) Shut down the equipment and have safety guards installed immediately.
   d) Fire the foreman.

5. You are about to be promoted and you have been told to recommend a successor to your job from the three men reporting to you. Whom do you select?
   a) Candidate A is 26 years old with minimum experience. He has been appraised as a "Doer" and every job he has tackled has been successful. However, his exposure to the overall operation has been minimal.
   b) Candidate B is 35 years old, has had broad exposure to the operations and has been characterized as "A good planner and organizer, but on some occasions the implementation of his plans has not been as good as it should be, although his overall record is fairly good."
   c) Candidate C is 58 years old, has been a successful contributor to the organization and knows how to get a job done. He is looking forward to early retirement at age 60.
6. You are a Materials Handling Manager and your department has 300 people, all salaried. The labor bargaining unit has just negotiated a contract which gives the production wage group an immediate 10 percent hike in base pay. The salaried group, which is non-union, will now earn less than the wage group. Merit review time for salaried employees is quickly approaching. Normally, salaried raises amount to 4%, with a maximum of 10% going to outstanding contributors. Your company management has not issued any new salaried employees raise policy, although they are aware that there now exists an uncomfortable distance between wage and salary earnings. They decide to let you make the decision, provided that you stay within the 4%-10% salary increase guidelines previously established. Your dilemma is this: You do not want your salaried people unionized. If you don't keep pace with wage earnings, however, unionization is a strong possibility.

On the other hand, an across-the-board increase would not reward superior performers. But to keep current with the wage group the full 10% is needed. How do you handle this one?

a) Give everyone a 10% increase.

b) Give normal performance a 4% increase, above average performance 7%, and outstanding performance 10%.

c) Give everyone a 4% increase and announce that company policy will be reviewed for possibility of a later across-the-board increase.

7. You are applying for a managerial position in a new company. Your record in the past has been successful and your current employer has the greatest regard for you. You are confident that the new position is one you can handle and make substantial contributions to. The one real hangup in your record is that you never completed college, being drafted into the Army the first semester of your junior year. The company you want to join has a mandatory requirement of college graduate for its managerial positions. After several discussions with the personnel people at the new company, you realize that while they may conduct reference checks with your former employers, they probably will not investigate your college record. What do you do?

a) Confess that you are not a college graduate.

b) Bluff your way through.

c) Confess that you are not a college graduate, but tell the personnel man that you intend to go to night school to get your degree.

8. You are a graduate mechanical engineer who has had five years experience as a supervisor in the product engineering section of a metal fabricator at $15,000 per year. You have been looking for a new job with greater opportunities. You are ambitious and

thoroughly enjoy product engineering work. You have received several job offers and have narrowed your choices to a select few where your opportunities for advancement look very good. Which one do you finally choose?

a) Company A manufactures textiles. You will be a department manager in production at $18,000 per year. Your boss would be a former wage worker who came up the hard way. He is tough and aggressive but doesn't readily accept nor understand new ideas.

b) Company B is a pharmaceutical house. You will be a manager of the plant maintenance force at $17,800 per year. Your boss here looks like he would be easy to handle.

c) Company C is a small metal fabricator and you would manage its product engineering department at $18,500 per year. There is no real "chemistry" between the boss and you.

d) Company D is also a metal fabricator but a large one. At $17,000 per year you would work as supervisor of product engineering. There is excellent chemistry between the boss and yourself, and the boss is due to retire in one year.

9. You are a Director of Sales enjoying a well deserved vacation in Miami for two weeks. During the third day of your vacation you receive a telephone call from the sales manager assigned your job while you are on vacation. He informs you that recent sales figures indicate a fairly large drop in sales for a prime district. How do you handle the situation?

a) Hang-up the phone.

b) Fly back to company headquarters immediately.

c) Tell your number two man to handle the situation, and if he can't, then get hold of you.

d) Call the Sales Manager of the affected sales district and discuss the situation.

10. A member of your peer group, a man who is also your close friend, drops in your office, closes the door, and tells you that he has heard from a reliable source that you are going to be fired from the company. What do you do?
   a) Nothing.
   b) Make a thorough but secretive check with some of your other friends to see if they have heard anything.
   c) Confront your boss immediately.
   d) Start sending out resumes.
   e) Resign from the company.

Now go on to the next section and see how well you've done.

Problem 1: The Product That's Going to Bomb

Let's consider your available responses. If you say nothing you're casting your fate to the winds. The same thing is true if you leave the situation in the hands of top management. Contrary to the Litany of Management, these fellows aren't omniscient; in fact, they probably know less about the new product than you. That's one of the reasons why they hired you, to help the company make the right decisions on new products. However, you cannot afford to be considered "negative." The company desperately needs new products, and you must take every measure to avoid criticism of being negative—while protecting your flanks. That's why you can't openly disclaim the product. The best response is alternative (d). Suggest that the product would enhance its chances for success by turning it over to Research for an extensive pilot plant run and have the Accounting boys estimate product costs. This response has two important consequences. First, it throws the project back in the lap of Research where it rightfully belongs. Those people have the responsibility of developing not only the product but the process; nd the process must be both feasible and economical. Second, the Accounting Department will estimate costs, and they will quickly unmask the hidden manufacturing costs.

At this stage, top management will hold Research responsible for developing the product fully and you are off the hook.

Reference: Corporate do-gooders (p. 77).

Problem 2: The Engineer Who Can't Work With People

The new engineer has been on the job for one year now. He has not proved capable of handling the job. Transferring him to another segment of the business relieves you of this particular headache, but someone else in your company must still face the problem. This is not the answer. The man has not adequately responded to counseling, and as we have come to see, human relations courses are too often ineffective, so that alternative is not feasible. Keeping him on will hurt your chances to do your assigned job. The *only* way to solve this unhappy problem is to fire the engineer. You are actually helping the man—at least, in the long run—by making him aware that he is obligated to step up to his responsibilities. You must be aware, too, that your primary responsibility is to get the job done. If you have someone in your organization that can't hold up his end, then he must be let go.

References: Firing people (176), Demand excellence (187).

Problem 3: The Loving Secretary

Unless you feel like shooting yourself for being such a damned ass, the answer to Problem 3 is (e), "None of the above." Actually, there is no "good" answer. You should never have permitted yourself to get into this ridiculous spot to begin with. If you're obsessed with the notion to play around, you had first better make sure that your livelihood isn't affected.

Reference: Managers and mistresses (p. 33).

Problem 4: Operating Without Safety Guards

The answer should be obvious, even painfully so. Shut down the equipment and have safety guards installed immediately. The foreman should also be disciplined for allowing an unsafe piece of equipment to be operated. He has too little regard for human life. You might even be better off if you fired him.

Reference: Safety can't wait (p. 14).

Problem 5: Picking a Successor

Let's consider Candidate B first. His record has only been fair to good. This is not enough, at least for the next upward level in the organization. If you promote mediocre performers, you'll get mediocre results. Candidate B has had several years to prove his mettle, and it doesn't look as if he will ever be a prime contributor. Candidate C, on the other hand, has done a good job for you. Unfortunately, he is not only close to retirement but anxiously awaiting it. Candidate A is the remaining man. His experience has been light, but every job he has tackled has been successful. That's a good sign. Given time and opportunity he will gain the necessary experience and will probably be an outstanding contributor. Since the organization will rally around a winner, he should be your choice. There is another option. You might elect to let Candidate C run the department for next two years, thereby giving candidate A an opportunity to broaden his experience. Candidate C has done a good job for you and will probably continue to do well in a new job. Candidate A, in the meantime, will recognize that the older man has but two years to go and he will probably bide his time, waiting to see if he gets the top job when the older man retires.

Reference: Selecting the best people for promotion (p. 175).

Problem 6: Pay Raise for the Salaried Group

All the alternatives in this case stink, but alternative (a) "Give everyone a 10 percent increase" is the least harmful. Actually, the company would have been smart to award some manner of across-the-board increase to maintain the level of salaried earnings with those of wage earnings. It could then have permitted some additional money to be awarded to salaried people of normal or above normal performance. This solution is the most equitable, and would have kept the salaried group content.

Since your company management obviously lacks foresight, and because they have not stepped up to their responsibility of creating an equitable earnings situation between the wage and salaried groups, it is now your responsibility to do the best job possible. Alternatives (b) and (c) will most certainly generate discontent and probably cause your people to unionize. Alternative (a) will at least keep your salaried group earnings at the level of wage earnings, although this still may not be enough to keep unionization away from your doorstep.

Good Luck!

References: Paychecks come first (p. 120), Scrooge and the pay raise (p. 118).

Problem 7: The College Degree

Most certainly you will not want to bare your soul and confess that you are not a college graduate, letting it go at that. That would be the kiss of death. You would not be considered for any managerial opening. On the other hand, you might consider mentioning that you never finished college but are going to attend night school until you possess that all-valuable sheepskin. Some companies will respect you for your determination and aggressiveness. Tragically, these companies are few. Most of the companies I have been associated with place an inordinate value on a college degree and will not give a second glance to a man who doesn't have a degree, even though he is attending night school and is close to finishing his required studies. This senseless attitude, and it only can be called that, has kept innumerable companies from obtaining men who are achievers. I have seen this narrow attitude in many personnel men, but I am still amazed whenever I encounter such inanity. No matter what the Litany of Management says, men without degrees are in many instances more aggressive and productive than men with degrees. They have to be—they're fighting an uphill battle. If you "smell" this biased attitude when you are being interviewed, your sale option is (b), bluff your way through—but only if you really feel that this is "the job" for you. I won't deny that this approach is loaded with risks. That it is. But if you can get on the job and prove your worth, and then the company discovers that you lied about the degree, chances are they will ignore it. Nothing succeeds like success, and companies need all the achievers they can get. There are too damn few good men around with or without college degrees. Don't permit an outdated bias to stand in your way.

References: Hiring people (p. 173), Mating of man and company (p. 131), Ethics in business? (p. 42).

Problem 8: Picking a New Job

At first glance, the obvious choice appears to be option (c), a small metal fabricator where you would manage the product engineering department at $18,500 per year, a nice increase over your current salary and a promotion from supervisor to manager. But there's a real hooker involved. There is no "chemistry" between you and the boss. Unless you can *safely* anticipate support from another executive in that company, you would be wise to forget this option. The cards are stacked against you right from the start, and at the first sign of serious trouble within your department, your boss may just leave you holding the bag. Similarly, alternative (a) would put you in a position of reporting to a boss where conflict might soon develop. He is a man who doesn't appreciate new ideas, and any aggressive proposals you make could easily be thwarted. You have another strike against you; you don't have production experience and you are unfamiliar with textiles. Since you will be expected to produce early in the game, your relative inexperience in both of these will count against you. Remember, you want to make as fast a start as possible. You now have reduced the options to two offers: the pharmaceutical house and the large metal fabricator. Now, you do not know pharmaceuticals. Neither have you had experience in plant maintenance. On the other hand, option (d) is directly in your field, product engineering. There is an excellent rapport between you and the boss, and he is due to retire in one year. This looks like the opportunity you have been waiting for. You know metal fabrication and you realize that you can make an immediate contribution on the job. Although the starting salary is only $17,000 per year, you know you will have an excellent chance of getting the top job within one year. Make this company your choice.

References: Mating of man and company (p. 131), Do you like your company's products? (p. 136), Compatability with the boss (p. 54), Angels (p. 57).

Problem 9: Emergency During Vacation

Make the sales manager step up to his responsibilities. Since he has been assigned your job while you are on vacation, he should be making the decisions. If he can't handle the job, or if he is unable to make decisions, he doesn't deserve a chance at the next upward step in the organization. This is a good opportunity to measure the man's depth. Tell him to handle the situation in his own way, and if he can't, then let him call you back. If he makes the decision himself, and makes the right one, you'll find out when you return to the job. Then you know you have a real comer in the organization. If he calls back for you to make the decision, then you have his number. In all fairness, let me state that it may be hard for you, as director of the organization, to throw the decision back in his lap. Remember, however, that people grow only when they are permitted to make decisions themselves. Resist the impulse to tell him how the situation should be handled. Select option (c).

References: Management by objectives (p. 181), Some thoughts on mistakes (p. 154).

Problem 10: Rumor From a Reliable Source

This is an old gambit of the cutthroat. Pretending friendship and concern for you, his old buddy, he viciously plants a rumor designed to hurl you into drastic and fatal action. For one reason or another, he is out to get you and he is counting on you to do something foolish in response to the rumor—such as confronting the boss immediately, sending out resumes, or resigning from the company. If you do anything so ridiculous, you have fallen into the cutthroat's trap. On the other hand, if you do nothing, you may never get peace of mind. Unless you are quite sure that the rumor is false and aimed to hurt you, check quietly with some of your close friends and confidants. If the rumor is false, which it most probably is, you have gained valuable knowledge about the cutthroat. In the future you will be able to watch him closely, and he won't be able to spring any surprises on you. A cutthroat who is recognized as such has lost his edge—which is vicious surprise. You will know how to play him and effectively counter his moves.

References: Sizing-up the cutthroat: guerrilla warfare (p. 45), Infighting (p. 49).

Epilogue: I Hate to See a Manager Cry

There is no happy ending to this book. Talk with any executive, manager or supervisor and he will find it exceedingly difficult to say that his life in the corporate halls has been one of relative tranquility. Listen to his personal stories of life on the job and you will find pain, anger, struggle, victory, defeat, and anguish.

It doesn't have to be that way—at least not all of the time. That is not to say that business is the most fun a person can have with his clothes on. Certainly, if a manager were sufficiently wealthy he wouldn't subject himself needlessly to the battering of corporate strife. Unfortunately, most people are forced to work. The successful ones will adapt themselves to the work environment as painlessly as possible. Those managers who approach their jobs with a full understanding of the duplicity of the Litany of Management will be better able to cope with the pressures they encounter.

The manager who will not play the game of business by its own long-established rules is unlikely to advance. He will be lucky if he holds on to his job and avoids stress illness.

The importance of business in our lives should not be permitted to blind us to its impersonal nature. The manager can only seek to remove the obstacles in his path by the manipulation of the power at his command. Anyone who approaches these formidable roadblocks naively or unknowledgeably may soon find himself working in a mood of anxiety and strain—a mood which, if prolonged, can wreck his morale and health.

It is important to erect a bulwark against the onset of stress situations in business. Knowledge of the real business code and recognition of the innumerable fallacies inherent in the Litany of Management can be powerful protection, for the realistic thinker dispels the misleading concepts which damage his career and subsequently his health.

I hope that this book has, at the very least, broadened your awareness of the realities of business life. That awareness is a major first step. The rest is in your hands. You should now be able to approach each business situation with a fresh perspective, a perspective that should enable you to increase your effectiveness on the job.

I can wish you only the very best, because goddammit, I hate to see a manager cry.